S. Hrg. 112–868

# ROUNDTABLE: THE FUTURE OF EMPLOYMENT FOR PEOPLE WITH THE MOST SIGNIFICANT DISABILITIES

# HEARING

OF THE

## COMMITTEE ON HEALTH, EDUCATION, LABOR, AND PENSIONS

## UNITED STATES SENATE

ONE HUNDRED TWELFTH CONGRESS

FIRST SESSION

ON

EXAMINING THE FUTURE OF EMPLOYMENT FOR PEOPLE WITH THE MOST SIGNIFICANT DISABILITIES

SEPTEMBER 15, 2011

Printed for the use of the Committee on Health, Education, Labor, and Pensions

Available via the World Wide Web: http://www.gpo.gov/fdsys/

U.S. GOVERNMENT PRINTING OFFICE

87–416 PDF        WASHINGTON : 2014

For sale by the Superintendent of Documents, U.S. Government Printing Office
Internet: bookstore.gpo.gov   Phone: toll free (866) 512–1800; DC area (202) 512–1800
Fax: (202) 512–2250   Mail: Stop SSOP, Washington, DC 20402–0001

# CONTENTS

---

## STATEMENTS

### THURSDAY, SEPTEMBER 15, 2011

# THE FUTURE OF EMPLOYMENT FOR PEOPLE WITH THE MOST SIGNIFICANT DISABILITIES

## THURSDAY, SEPTEMBER 15, 2011

U.S. SENATE,
COMMITTEE ON HEALTH, EDUCATION, LABOR, AND PENSIONS,
*Washington, DC.*

The committee met, pursuant to notice, at 10:04 a.m. in Room 106, Dirksen Senate Office Building, Hon. Tom Harkin, chairman of the committee, presiding.

Present: Senators Harkin, Mikulski, Merkley, and Franken.

### OPENING STATEMENT OF SENATOR HARKIN

The CHAIRMAN. The Senate Committee on Health, Education, Labor, and Pensions will come to order. Last week, President Obama made an impassioned plea for the Congress to focus our attention on the jobs crisis in America. On Tuesday, the Census Bureau reported that nearly one in six Americans were living in poverty, with the number increasing each year for the last 4 years. Even more depressing is that about one in four children in America are now living in poverty. I might remind people that the poverty level for a family of four, two adults and two children, is about $22,000 a year. That's about $425 a month.

The number of Americans in severe poverty is also going up, and that is those living at or less than half of the poverty rate. That means a family of four making $11,000 a year or less. That's how bad things are.

Unemployment is stubbornly holding over 9 percent. I think the President is correct that we've got to move ahead on a jobs bill. But today we'll focus the HELP Committee's attention on an often overlooked piece of the employment problem, or unemployment problem, and that's the shockingly low labor force participation of workers with disabilities.

According to the Bureau of Labor Statistics, as of August there were more than 15 million adults with disabilities in the United States between the ages of 16 and 64, working age. Of this group, less than one-third were participating in the labor force; over two-thirds not working. So you say, "OK, the unemployment rate in America is 9 percent, but the unemployment rate for people with significant disabilities is about 60 percent, 60 to 66 percent."

In the last 3 years, statistics show us that people with disabilities have been leaving the labor force at a rate of more than 10 times the rate of the nondisabled population. In other words, as people have been laid off and jobs decreasing, those with disabilities are being let go at a rate 10 times that of the nondisabled population.

This is unacceptable. I might even go so far as to say I think this is gross discrimination. We need to take action to change this trend.

This roundtable today is meant to look ahead. I am an optimist at heart. I do believe that we will be coming out of the recession, that we will increase employment. The gears will start to work, sooner, I hope, rather than later. I just want to make sure that as employment starts to go up, that if the people with disabilities have been leaving the labor force at 10 times the rate of the nondisabled, they should be rehired at 10 times the rate of people without disabilities.

I want to look ahead and think about how we set up systems and do things that really get people with disabilities employed in gainful employment. For today's roundtable I want to focus on an important element of the disability community, people who have significant disabilities and who often experience multiple barriers to employment.

In March, we held a HELP Committee hearing focused on people with intellectual disabilities, and some of the biggest barriers to success in the labor market for people with significant disabilities are what? Low expectations, discriminatory attitudes, lack of early life preparation for gainful employment, and I think just, quite frankly, a failure of imagination on how we can construct systems for gainful employment for people with significant disabilities.

The purpose today is to hear from a diverse group of experts about how they would improve our education, our workforce development, our human service programs, so that people with the most significant disabilities who want to work are able to find a place in the labor market and have a career that works for them.

It's often said that it's not enough just to give someone a job that's a dead-end street. There's got to be some hope for improvement and advancement as life progresses.

I'm working with Ranking Member Enzi and other members of the committee to use this roundtable and other hearings to inform a multiyear disability employment initiative. My goal is to make the policy changes necessary, engage with leaders in the business and disability community so that the size of the disability workforce will grow from 4.9 million to 6 million by 2015. We sort of set that goal, but that's not just mine. The U.S. Chamber of Commerce has also set that goal.

I want to make sure that we don't leave behind a community of people with significant disabilities and that they have to be brought along as part of that increase. As we approach today's topic, I want to keep in mind the diversity of needs and experiences in the disability community. For purposes of today's discussion, I'm focused on people with the most significant disabilities because they don't always benefit from traditional disability employment strategies. For example, some sources have estimated that the labor force participation rate for people with intellectual disabilities is below 25 percent; for people with severe and persistent mental illness, below 10 percent.

Moreover, I believe that policies that work for people with the most significant disabilities—let me repeat that—polices that work for people with the most significant disabilities, things like workplace flexibility, assistance with starting, early involvement in secondary school, sustaining micro-enterprises, tailoring the elements of a job to the capacities and interests of the worker, when you look at all those, those also benefit workers with less severe disabilities, or even people without disabilities, sort of like universal design. Universal design helps everybody.

In addition, people with the most significant disabilities have the highest participation rates in our most expensive safety net programs—Medicare, Medicaid, Social Security Disability Insurance, SSI—which means if we're successful in helping this population achieve some economic self-sufficiency, then we have some savings on the government side.

Senators Murray, Enzi, Isakson and I have been working on a bipartisan reauthorization of what we call WIA, the Workforce Investment Act, and we've sought to make changes in the Vocational Rehabilitation title of that bill to strengthen VR's emphasis on competitive, integrated employment, and prioritize services for young people with disabilities as they enter the workforce for the first time.

Today's roundtable hopefully will inform our ongoing efforts to reauthorize the Workforce Investment Act, to spur new thinking that can inform other legislative efforts like the President's jobs bill, and other bills.

Let me introduce our panel and we'll kick it off.

Ruby Moore is the executive director of the Georgia Advocacy Office, which is the P&A, protection and advocacy agency for people with disabilities in Georgia. Ms. Moore has worked for 35 years advocating for and running competitive, integrated employment programs for people with significant disabilities. Thank you for being here.

Next we have Katy Beh Neas, vice president for Government Relations for Easter Seals. Katy is a disability policy expert representing a national network of Easter Seals affiliates that operate a wide range of employment programs for people with significant disabilities. I might add that in her earlier life she was a member of our staff on this committee.

Michael Pearson is the president and majority shareholder of Union Packing, LLC in Yeadon, PA. Mr. Pearson brings a perspective of a successful small business owner who has made a real effort to hire a diverse workforce, including people with disabilities. Thank you for being here.

Next we have Julie Petty of Fayetteville, AR, a national leader in the self-advocate movement. She is past president of the Self Advocates Becoming Empowered, a national membership organization that brings the first- person perspective of individuals with significant disabilities to public policy discussions. Julie currently works at Partners for Inclusive Communities, the Arkansas University Center of Excellence in Developmental Disabilities. Thank you for being here.

And Deb Pumphrey of Ottumwa, IA is the parent of a 27-year-old with multiple and complex disabilities. Deb is a parent-leader and advocate in Iowa who has worked hard to find employment that works for her son. She currently chairs the board of Tenco Industries, which operates a community-based recycling program that employs her son and other people with significant disabilities in the Ottumwa area. Thank you for being here.

Next we have Janet Samuelson, the executive director of ServiceSource, an agency that serves people with disabilities in nine states and the District of Columbia. Ms. Samuelson brings over 35 years of experience in the disability field and leads a nonprofit that provides employment and day treatment, training and support services to over 19,000 individuals. Thank you for being here.

And Fred Schroeder. Fred is not here yet. He's en route. Well, I'll introduce him even though he's en route. Dr. Fred Schroeder is an expert in vocational rehabilitation, having served as the Commissioner of the Rehabilitation Services Administration under former President Clinton. Dr. Schroeder took steps during his tenure at RSA to make clear that the goal of the public vocational rehab program is competitive, integrated employment, and to hold rehabilitation counselors accountable for achieving that goal.

And, last but not least, we have Dr. Jonathan Young, who currently serves as chair of the National Council on Disability, an independent Federal agency advising Congress and the President on public policy. Dr. Young brings a perspective of an attorney and historian who has chronicled the history of the disability rights movement and has advocated for policies that advance the goals of the Americans with Disabilities Act, equality of opportunity, full participation, independent living, and economic self-sufficiency. Thank you for being here, Jonathan.

Thank you all for being here. I'd like to now begin what I hope will be an open, free flowing discussion on this issue. I'd like to lay out two topics to organize our conversation.

First, what is the right spectrum of employment options that will address the needs of workers with the most significant disabilities?

Second, what are the best proven strategies for workers with the most significant disabilities to increase their earnings over time and achieve career advancement?

To help frame the conversation, I want to offer a working definition, I hope, and I can be corrected or this can be amended by anyone here. But what is a working definition of "the most significant disabilities" in the context of employment? For purposes of today's discussion, I would suggest that people with the most significant disabilities are people for whom competitive employment has not traditionally occurred, has been interrupted, or is intermittent because of the disability; or who, because of the severity of the disability, need intensive or extended support services to work competitively. Now, if you have other views on that and other things to add, maybe I didn't cover it all.

We have our introductions. I laid out the two sort of broad areas that I would like to discuss, and I'd just reiterate one of them. What's the right spectrum of employment options that will address the needs of workers with the most significant disabilities?

I will open questioning with Julie Petty. Before we talk about the spectrum of employment options, Ms. Petty, what goal should we have regarding employment for people with disabilities, especially those with the most significant disabilities? What goals should we have? From your perspective as someone who has a disability, who advocates, what is it that we should be striving for? That's a sort of general, open-ended question.

### STATEMENT OF JULIE PETTY, PAST PRESIDENT, SELF-ADVOCATES BECOMIMG EMPOWERED, FAYETTEVILLE, AR

Ms. PETTY. Thank you for having me today. I think you talked a little bit about it earlier when you talked about the discrimination. First we have to change attitudes about people with intellectual and developmental disabilities. We have to think that everyone can work. Now, that might not be the same for all people with disabilities, but everyone can work.

We have sheltered workshops all over the Nation. I know a lot of my friends work there, and they've been there for many, many years because people don't believe in them. People don't think they can do much, but they've never been given the opportunity, and I really do believe it's an attitude change. If the attitude changes, then the service system for the employers and even from ourselves, we have to believe in ourselves. We know that the sheltered workshop model is an outdated model and that things can be done differently. Everyone can work means that people have individual employment plans.

I would like to share with you a story about a woman in Oregon who was in a sheltered workshop, and she has severe, significant disabilities. She uses a wheelchair, and all she did all day is bang her fist on the table and yell. Well, somebody got a clue and decided this might not be the best place for her. So they found a factory in Oregon and they created a customized button that she could hit that would run the machine, and she could yell all she wanted because nobody else could hear her. That is one place that we need to think outside the box.

The CHAIRMAN. That's why I kind of referred to it as having imagination.

Ms. PETTY. Yes, sir. And I would also like to share with you another reason why we should strive for employment for people and that is because of quality of life. If you have a real job, you've got real money. I have friends with significant disabilities who don't get to go to the movies, who don't get to go many places. And then you have the service providers who work for these organizations who go off to the Caribbean or wherever they want to go. So the quality of life overall is healthy. It's healthier for people to have a job.

I've been in many sheltered workshops all over the Nation, and people aren't smiling, people aren't happy. One of my friends in Arkansas, his sister got mad because he got food out of the snack machine all the time. Well, he doesn't have a lot to do during the day, so he goes to the snack machine.

When we have a real job and we have employment that is integrated—we also can develop relationships. I have a lot of friends with disabilities, but I have a lot of friends without disabilities too, and I met them through work and through other organizations.

When we are able to contribute to society, that's just another way for us to be treated with dignity and respect, and Americans with disabilities deserve to be treated with dignity and respect. And those are just some of the ways we can help people get integrated employment and be happy and live a happy life. Thanks.

The CHAIRMAN. I'm going to move from you right to your neighbor to your left. Deb, you're the mother of a son with significant disabilities. I think Ms. Petty just made a very profound statement about work and the quality of life and friendships, all the things that go with having employment that challenges you and gives you a pathway upward.

Again, what are our goals, or what are our expected goals for employing persons with significant disabilities? What should we be looking at? What kind of goals—or if that's not the right question for you, just go ahead and tell us how you feel about this.

## STATEMENT OF DEB PUMPHREY, PARENT ADVOCATE, OTTUMWA, IA

Ms. PUMPHREY. Thank you for having me here today, first of all. And second, I guess my goal always for my son, who has significant intellectual disabilities, was for him to work in our community. I have come to realize, though, that without the significant and intensive amount of support that he would need, he is not able to do that. He functions at about a 4- to 5-year-old level, and to have a person with that level of intellectual disability working in the community without the intensive support just has not been possible with Joshua.

He works in a sheltered workshop, and I believe that that spectrum of employment needs to be there for persons with significant disabilities, just for the support that he requires. Inside the sheltered workshop he does have employment. He is shredding paper on a pretty regular basis with a one-on-one staff person that I am able to employ through the Consumer Choice Options Program through the Intellectual Disabilities Waiver. So he has his one-on-one support person who is there a few hours a week for him to have employment.

We've had to be creative in how we've looked at his employment opportunity, and I'm here to tell you that the difference in the quality of his life as a result of that few hours a week of employment is significantly different. We've seen a reduction in his behavior problems. He's just extremely content with life at this point. So just a few hours a week have made a very significant difference in his life, and in order to do that we've had to be creative and look outside the box.

The CHAIRMAN. How long has he been doing this? How long has he been at the workshop?

Ms. PUMPHREY. He's been at the workshop since he graduated from high school, so about 5 years.

The CHAIRMAN. Five years?

Ms. PUMPHREY. Yes. We've been able to do the employment from inside the workshop for probably about a year. We had to get creative.

The CHAIRMAN. OK. Thank you.

I already introduced Dr. Fred Schroeder. Welcome. I'm sorry you got held up someplace, wherever that was. I don't know if it was traffic, but things do get held up around here. But welcome, Dr. Schroeder, we just started our panel discussion.

I just want to say again, I kind of want a free-flowing discussion. I don't want to have to always jump in and recognize somebody. If you have something to add, if you want to say something, we have an old process here where you just take your nameplate and turn it up like that, and I'll call on you.

We're coming back to Ms. Petty right away.

I want to get other people involved in this discussion now. Go ahead.

Ms. PETTY. I just wanted to make a point to Ms. Pumphrey, one of the reasons her son has that support in the workshop, why can't we spend the money to get him support in the community? Because there are many recycling areas, and I'm just wondering why did there have to be a segregated place?

The CHAIRMAN. OK. Your question basically is if Deb's son needs all the supportive services for—was it 4 days a week or something you said?

Ms. PUMPHREY. He's only working about 2 hours a week, actually.

The CHAIRMAN. If he needs all that for a sheltered employment, you're saying why shouldn't he have that supportive services for nonsheltered employed?

Ms. PETTY. Right.

The CHAIRMAN. OK, fair question. Any observations on that? Again, I'm still getting back to the right spectrum of employment options. I'll be provocative here. There are some who are saying we should have no sheltered employment whatsoever. There are others that say that sheltered employment is a necessary part of a spectrum of different employment opportunities.

What we're trying to do here and what I'm trying to do in the WIA bill is to change the default position. The default position for people with significant intellectual disabilities in the past has been sheltered workshops. I want to change that default position so that it is integrated competitive employment.

However, there may be some who, through their own choice, their family choice, their own individual choice, may feel more comfortable, more fulfilled in sheltered employment. Who am I to deny that to someone that may feel more of a kinship there, more of an ability to grow, and maybe we need to talk to those that have sheltered workshops. I don't know. I don't know all the functioning of it, but get them to provide pathways of growth for people that are working there.

And since we've talked about that, I don't know who had theirs up first, but I'll go with Mrs. Moore, and then I'll go with Ms. Neas.

### STATEMENT OF RUBY MOORE, EXECUTIVE DIRECTOR, GEORGIA ADVOCACY OFFICE, DECATUR, GA

Ms. MOORE. Thank you, Senator Harkin. I appreciate the perspectives of my two colleagues so far, and maybe I can help a little bit to bridge the gap.

I think when we're trying to advance in anything, we're trying to make things better, we're trying to help people have good lives, trying to actually have a piece of the American dream, the American way, that we start with what we know and we start with our strengths. And our strengths, what we know is that people with very significant disabilities are working in the community, are working in competitive and integrated jobs, real jobs for meaningful wages.

We know that, and we have decades of research and demonstration now of what people are capable of, and I'm well aware that often we have knowledge in our field from an individual perspective about how to go about supporting people with very significant disabilities to have great jobs that isn't necessarily common knowledge across all of the communities where people live and may not be immediately available.

But what we do know is that we've just learned a lot that allows us to say we really don't need to create special places for people with disabilities that are segregated and that are paying sub-minimum wages. I don't say that lightly, and I recognize that if we're moving away from that, we have to do that in a very planful, measured, careful way to not create an adverse impact on people, and for people to actually have real choices.

One of the problems with heavily investing in segregation is that it takes away choices for people. So I'll just speak very briefly on some of the things we've learned. We've learned a lot in the last 35 years. If we're talking about sub-minimum wages, we've learned a lot in the last 73 years.

The CHAIRMAN. Right.

Ms. MOORE. Some of the ideas that got advanced in order to let veterans returning from World War I coming back to an industrial manufacturing economy don't necessarily hold today as what people with significant disabilities need. But we've learned a lot about how to discover what people are good at, what they love, as I like to say what makes people sparkle and shine, their unique contributions, their interests, their talents, their support needs, the environments in which people do well. We've learned a lot in terms of the advances with assistive technology.

You talked about workplace flexibility, Senator. I think you're precisely on point with that. We've learned a lot about how to customize and negotiate relationships between potential employees with significant disabilities, even just people who have a very limited frame of reference for choosing work or knowing what they want to do, and employers who have unmet needs, even in this economy, and being able to blend those two, those relationships together in a way that works for the employer and the employee.

And, Senator, to your point, you're precisely right. I'm an employer. Seventy-eight percent of my employees have disabilities, and the very things that we do to performance enhancements, restructuring the environment, creating jobs that meet our needs but I didn't have a job description for before I met the person who could do it, it's that kind of inventive and imaginative process that allows the entire workforce to do better, not just the person with a significant disability.

I'll just move along because I know everybody wants to talk. But I would like to just say that when we're thinking of a spectrum of services or options, I don't think the spectrum should be predicated on an old notion that people aren't ready to work. People are ready to work. And even in this economy, employers still have unmet needs.

When I think of the spectrum, I think what's culturally normative, even culturally valued. How did any of us learn what we were interested in, what we might be able to do, how we might be able to make a unique contribution? I know that I didn't grow up saying I think I'll be a protection and advocacy system director. I don't know when you decided or discovered or figured out that you wanted to be a U.S. Senator and to shape national policy and help Americans have good lives, but I suspect it was a whole series of life experiences.

The spectrum begins, as you pointed out, it's a lifespan kind of spectrum. It's not a spectrum of boxes that we have to move through in order to finally get a real job. You start with supporting young people and their families early on to say what's the best way to teach my child with a disability, along with my other children if I have other children, how to have a work ethic? It begins by doing chores. It begins by getting support to say how do I include my child with a significant disability to be part of this family in a way that they have responsibilities? That's how you start beginning a work ethic.

In school the teacher turns to certain kids and says will you help out with this. This is where people learn how to solve problems, work as a team. These are all the social skills you need in order to be successful on the job, which turns out to be more important even than being noticeably, objectively productive.

Then there are summer jobs and there are internships, and I think we should encourage and support schools to give people real-life work experiences regardless of type or level of disability before they graduate from school, and then to create that path to employment that doesn't begin with the presumption that you have to get ready. You will have been getting ready.

I think as we go on today we'll probably talk a lot about different kinds of models that have existed for a long time, and our best practices, customized employment, supported employment, which we'll talk more about probably, actually grew out of and on the shoulders of what people have learned in sheltered workshops. So we're not dismissive of services that have been around for a long time, but it is time to move beyond segregation and sub-minimum wages.

The CHAIRMAN. I want to ask Ms. Neas to respond also. But it seems that voc rehab that we've all been very supportive of, and they do a great job, but it came to my attention I guess in the last few years that voc rehab has been focused mostly on people with physical disabilities and has not been focused on young people with intellectual disabilities and working with them at an early stage. Like you say, the spectrum is not a bunch of boxes. It's sort of a continuum, and working with young people with intellectual disabilities to challenge them, to help them build their relationships, help them to think about what their future is going to be and what kind of work they want to do and what they might find challenging, what they're capable of doing, that's just all part of it, and we're trying to get voc rehab looking at that.

Ms. MOORE. Good.

The CHAIRMAN. Ms. Neas.

Ms. NEAS. Thank you.

The CHAIRMAN. You're so soft-spoken, you might pull that in, Katy, a little bit. There you go. Thanks.

## STATEMENT OF KATY BEH NEAS, SENIOR VICE PRESIDENT, GOVERNMENT RELATIONS, EASTER SEALS, OFFICE OF PUBLIC AFFAIRS, WASHINGTON, DC

Ms. NEAS. I want to just add a couple of things, and I totally agree with what everyone has said. I think one of the challenges, at least from my perspective, on this issue is I believe everybody's got a very valid point in this discussion.

For me the thing that's most important is we need to build on the investment that we've made in the early intervention and special education services that many of these young people have gained. Are they getting what they need from the school system to make them ready for the world of work? I would argue, unfortunately in too many instances, the answer is no.

We are seeing in our programs kids that are exiting the school system without the ability to have an understanding of the concept of productivity and that if you're going to be successful in an integrated community-based setting, you need to be able to demonstrate the productivity as another person who could do the same job.

The CHAIRMAN. You mean exiting the school system.

Ms. NEAS. Right. And the other thing that we're hearing from our affiliates is this concept of taking feedback and instruction from your supervisor, that those are two places that we're seeing kids coming out of school not having the skill set that they need, and that's something that we really want to have be a part of their education before they leave.

The other thing we have seen over time, and I think especially in the last 20 years, a whole change of expectations about what people with disabilities can and cannot do, starting in 1975 with the start of IDEA, where kids had a right to be in the school. In 1997, we clarified that right. That meant you had the right to be taught the same stuff as your nondisabled peers. What a concept. You could be there but not be educated. That still, unfortunately, was a challenge in 1997.

In 1986, we established the early intervention program, infants and toddlers getting a really good start, and the other thing of educating their parents that it was OK to have high expectations for their child. Again, it sounds simple to say now, but it was transformative. If you talk to parents whose kids have benefited from early intervention, as you and I did earlier this summer, kids that had very little skill sets when they were 1 and 2 that are high school graduates looking forward to their future, ideas about their careers, there's a connection between those two things, and we need to really enforce those concepts that we have to help families understand to have high expectations. We have to give kids the skills that they need to be successful, and that those are very important predictors for how they're going to be successful in the world of work.

I think the other thing I will say, and let other people talk, is this whole concept of job exploration and internships, and one of the things that especially a number of our affiliates are doing for kids that are leaving high school, trying to figure out what they want to do, spending a month over the course of 6 months in six different places to see do I like working at Kinko's, do I like working at a hospital, do I want to work in the grocery store. Most of us learn what we like by giving it a shot. That needs to be true for people with disabilities, and they need the supports that they need.

One of the things that we've been very frustrated with is finding internships for people who need very significant supports. It's one thing to find an internship for someone with a disability who just needs an accommodation. It's another thing for someone who needs the kinds of supports to do the job, and I think that's a place where we'd really like to see some leadership from employers to help make those opportunities more available.

And then I just did the math, and I had no idea what I wanted to do when I grew up, and I didn't really know it until I got an internship in my congressman's office in 1984, and that absolutely shaped my destiny. I would say for the rest of us, internships, job exploration was how we figured out what we liked to do and whether or not we had any aptitude in it, and I think that's something you don't know until you try, and I really think we need to create more opportunities for people to be able to try more things with the supports that they need to be successful.

The CHAIRMAN. Very good. I want to talk about that program that we looked at this summer, because that's what it was, young people trying different things.

I want to go to Mr. Pearson. But before I do that, I want to recognize again someone that has just, for all the years I've known Senator Mikulski, even when she was a congresswoman, I didn't know you in Baltimore, but I knew you when you came to Congress. She's just been someone who has been one of the great supporters of moving the concept of how we treat people with disabilities, how we integrate them in our schools, in our environment, providing work opportunities.

I'm just proud and privileged to be her friend, and she is the ranking person on this committee, Senator Barbara Mikulski.

### STATEMENT OF SENATOR MIKULSKI

Senator MIKULSKI. Thank you very much, Senator Harkin.

Picking up on what Kathy said, I'm sitting next to a legal aid lawyer. I'm a social worker, started out as a child welfare worker, but I didn't intend to do that when I was 9 years old. I saw a movie about Madame Curie, and I wanted to be a scientist, to win two Nobel Prizes and marry a Frenchman.

[Laughter.]

I kind of did that work that you said, which is try it out. I was klutzy in science but now fund a lot of the science programs. We're all friends, and I think we see this as a bit of the good news is that people with so-called disabilities are often underestimated in terms of their capability and their competency. There's a tendency to either ghettoize or want to feel sorry for people, and so much has changed, as you've said.

I want to thank Senator Harkin for his ongoing advocacy. And we need to look at how the fact that one size is not going to fit all in terms of our regs. I believe that the digital world, the digital economy has changed everything, providing opportunities for people that they might not have had in the analog or heavy-duty manufacturing world that our economy was once built on.

We are beyond the sheltered workshop. We're just beyond that now because our economy has changed, and I know from within my own State I have people with varying views. I love the fact that the National Federation of the Blind is headquartered in Maryland and in Baltimore. I love the fact that they picketed me to get my attention on this issue. As an old organizer, it was a great approach. And we need to look at the issues between people with one set of challenges in their life and in the others, particularly around issues like autism, intellectual disabilities, and chronic mental illness where there might be an ongoing history of schizophrenia.

What I see—and I'll just stop here—on one hand, by being on the Intelligence Committee, I've visited a variety of agencies, and boy, what a surprise, and here's the surprise, not that we weren't doing a good job to stop bad things from happening with us. But when I went to the National Geospatial Agency, our eye in the sky, there were a significant number of people with severe significant hearing loss that were there standing sentry to protect America. They didn't have to hear. They had to see. They were full-time employees, 12s, 14s, 15s, heading to the senior executive corps because of what they could do.

If you went to the National Security Agency, which is again our listening post on the world, our code-breaker monitor, there were people with significant visual impairments working there because they didn't have to see. They had to be able to hear, and they had to be able to do math to break the codes. Doing math had nothing to do with whether you could see or not.

And when I went to one of our private sector sites, as I looked at a mission control place, somebody couldn't get up to shake my hand because he'd had amputations because of wounds in Iraq, but he could still be there fighting on cyber security because he had the right training and the right stuff and was earning full-time wages to do a full-time job protecting America.

We're in a different world, and I'd just use that because you say, "well," but then at the same time we have people in our community and in our own families with autism, intellectual disabilities. They want to work. Work is often their most important part of self-identity, structure, and the ability to be independent, not only from a financial standpoint but that sense of competency.

So when we look at it, some are going to need help. Some might even need subsidies. Some might need subsidies through different kinds of wages. But I think Washington and the way we go about it, from vocational ed to vocational rehab, we are in a different economy. We need to seize the concepts of the economy and then make sure we are not still operating with a 1950 manufacturing analog mentality.

Between meds and the digital world and all the other things, I think we can have a breakthrough that is fair and just, and just listening to you is one inspiration, and I want to thank you for the work you do every day. It is inspirational leadership.

And then the other, how do we parse this, and in parsing it, we don't ghettoize.

Thank you for what you do, and let's work together and try to break this code of economic justice and economic reality.

The CHAIRMAN. Thank you very much, Senator Mikulski, social worker or legal aid lawyer.

Senator MIKULSKI. Born-again do-gooders.

[Laughter.]

The CHAIRMAN. You're right, I never thought I'd ever be a Senator.

[Laughter.]

Never heard of it at that time.

Mr. Pearson, here you are. You're a small business owner. You have a diverse workforce. We sort of got off it a little bit, but that's OK, the spectrum of opportunities and how you see it as a business owner yourself.

## STATEMENT OF MICHAEL PEARSON, PRESIDENT AND MAJORITY SHAREHOLDER OF UNION PACKING, LLC, YEADON, PA

Mr. PEARSON. First of all, thank you for inviting me. And I've had the misfortune or good fortune of having worked in corporate America, been a small business owner, and I've seen the spectrum, and I believe there are opportunities, and often we as business owners or leaders of businesses are not open to opportunities we can offer.

And to our advantage, we begin to open up and employ individuals, we get loyalty, we get folks who come to work on time, and we get a competitive group that add value to our enterprise. My experience, while I don't have experience with those with severe disabilities, I have been very successful employing individuals who had some learning differences.

Nineteen percent of my workforce—and we're 70 employees making fast-food packaging for some of the entities around the country. I'm sure you've all had some nuggets or some form of fast food in our packaging. My workforce, my managers, at first were very apprehensive, did not embrace bringing on these individuals, and were fearful. But with education and commitment we soon realized, wow, they can do the job, and they can do it well. And I think that fear and apprehension is met in several sectors of the employer spectrum, and it's important that education of employers, to go back to Ms. Petty's comments, that all of us need to learn something.

And in small business and mid-size business, we are especially equipped with the ability to make those accommodations and changes that can facilitate successful employment for individuals with disabilities.

The CHAIRMAN. Let me ask you this. Do any of the individuals that work for you require supportive services at any point during the workday? Do they require any kind of supportive services like Ms. Petty was talking about, or I think Ms. Pumphrey was also talking about? Just sometimes people might need a little bit of support during the day, not all the time but once in a while they might need something. Do you have anything like that?

Mr. PEARSON. My employees have not, but they have received support when they first entered my workforce, and that was the coaching and the direction and some of the soft skills that lead toward individuals being successful, and that is a burden lifted off of my HR department, where these are individuals that come ready to work. And often that's supported by nonprofits or some entity that comes in and allows me as a business owner to have a pool of talent where I know those things have been screened and they're coming work-ready, and that relieves some of the fear.

The CHAIRMAN. I have to make sure you meet Randy Lewis sometime with Walgreen's. That's a little bit bigger business than yours.

Mr. PEARSON. Yes, a little bit bigger than us.

The CHAIRMAN. But I remember he made the point here at a hearing that when they first started hiring people again with intellectual disabilities, that they always showed up at work on time, they were very productive because they could focus on one aspect of their job and become very productive on it.

On the physical disability side, I always use the example of my own brother who is now deceased but who was deaf, and Mr. Delavan, who had a manufacturing company in Des Moines in the early 1950s and started hiring deaf people. It was very noisy. Of course, that was before we had a lot of OSHA stuff and all that kind of stuff. So it was very noisy, but we found out that deaf people didn't care how noisy it was, and they could focus on these little machines and stuff that they were working on. They found them to be the most productive of their workers.

Mr. PEARSON. Senator, you're very right. As an employer, I should be concentrating on what people can do as opposed to what they can't do, and that begins to change my mind set. I can then farm for talent in places that are traditionally not areas we would look.

The CHAIRMAN. Ms. Neas raised an interesting point, and that is about early intervention. I think a couple of you mentioned it. You mentioned it, too, Ms. Moore, about early intervention programs, and also giving people the opportunity to explore different job opportunities. That's what you and I saw this summer. I was very enthralled by that, where they could experience internship programs and find something that fit them, they liked it, they could do it.

I think for many families with children with significant disabilities, it's tough enough just to get through the day and to get the kids to school, fight with the local school board to make sure that they get adequate instruction, and then a lot of high school kids have internships and do different things, but kids with significant disabilities hardly ever get that opportunity.

We need to be looking at ways, and that's where I'm hoping that voc rehab now can begin to focus on young people to get them those kind of internships in the summertime and things like that, after-school jobs, so that they can test a variety of different avenues.

Ms. NEAS. I think to add to that, Senator Harkin, is some of the things that Mr. Pearson said, having people have the skill set to be in a work environment, not only have the competency to do the job.

One of the things that we struggle with are people with significant autism or Asperger's who may be off the charts in terms of their intellectual abilities, you know, Ph.D. on top of Ph.D., but can't hold a job because they don't have the skill set, the personal human-to-human skill set. I think those are other things that are really important for us to make sure that kids leave high school having some guidance in that area so that appropriate behavior to the best of their ability is something that is a goal, and clearly there are going to be people for whom that is not going to be possible as a part of their disability. But I think trying to help those people who can acquire that skill is going to be very, very important.

We are also doing a lot of work with returning Afghanistan and Iraq veterans. Most of these folks, whether they've had a physical injury, because so many of them have had brain injuries, they've got a lot of issues they didn't have before their service. One of the concerns that was raised earlier was about flexibility within a job, and we've got a protocol we're working on with employers that says that person may not be able to be there every morning at 9 o'clock. Is there a way to structure the job so that they can do the job if they show up at 11:30 or at 1 o'clock? And please don't fire them if they're late 4 days in a row because that's part of what they're trying to figure out, how they're sleeping, how they're managing the morning routine, and that it's those sorts of things that I think they are bringing to the environment. It's not just a luxury that people need but it really is an accommodation that people who are navigating a whole new world for themselves need in order to make themselves financially stable.

The CHAIRMAN. I see Dr. Schroeder has his nameplate up. Fred, I recognize you.

## STATEMENT OF FRED SCHROEDER, Ph.D., FORMER COMMISSIONER OF THE REHABILITATION SERVICES ADMINISTRATION, DEPARTMENT OF EDUCATION, INTERWORK INSTITUTE, SAN DIEGO STATE UNIVERSITY, SAN DIEGO, CA

Mr. SCHROEDER. Thank you, Senator, and thank you for holding this discussion, but also for your many years of leadership in advancing the dignity and integration of people with disabilities.

As far as whether vocational rehabilitation under-serves youth with intellectual disabilities, I'm not familiar with any data to suggest that. There is a good bit of cooperation between vocational rehabilitation and school systems, and clearly transition is something that we all see as value-added and very important.

One thing that I would highlight is that during the 1998 amendments to the Rehabilitation Act, we added a provision that individuals who were receiving Social Security Disability Insurance or Supplemental Security income would be presumed eligible for vocational rehabilitation as a way of focusing the program on people who demonstrably have significant disabilities.

I'd like to speak just a moment to the issue of the spectrum of options. In my view—and, of course, it's a very complicated issue. But in my view, having segregated work settings does not enhance the options for employment for people with disabilities but constricts the options. And I say that because as long as society is allowed to believe that there is a place over there somewhere for those people, people with disabilities will continue to suffer misunderstanding, which leads to diminished opportunities for integrated employment.

I firmly believe in choice, but I do not believe that the majority of people who work in sheltered workshops are there out of choice. Clearly, there will be some. But when you have a two-thirds unemployment rate among adults with disabilities, a very difficult time finding integrated employment, and the only option that you can see available to you is a segregated facility, that's not choice. By definition, choice means options. And in order to facilitate those options, we have to look for creative ways to support integrated work.

I don't want to belabor this concept, but I'd like to add just one additional thing, the attitudes. One of the problems that people with disabilities face is that we are regarded as broken people. We're regarded as less capable by virtue of disability. I don't think people think it consciously, and I certainly don't think they mean it with any ill will. But what that means is if I go to a facility, the presumption is that I will likely be somewhere below the productivity standard by virtue of disability, and that I might, if I am very skilled and work very hard, I might get up to the productivity standard, but doing what kind of a job? A job that at its high end is still a very low-paid job.

I'm 54 years old. If I went to a facility and I was having to—I know of a facility that makes mattresses, and they're big and they're heavy, and as I say, my back is not what it used to be, would I be up to productivity? I don't know. Likelihood would be not. But even if I were, I'd be making $7.25 an hour.

The need for customized employment, the need for employment that does not emphasize the person's disability but the individual's strengths and interests, that is the underpinning of the real solution to the unemployment and under-employment of people with disabilities. And if I go to a facility and by nature of what contracts they have, they have two or three or four different jobs, that is such a narrow spectrum, and on top of that those jobs again, by and large, are very low skilled, low-wage jobs.

I believe that while there are people for whom segregated work is something that they value, I just want to reiterate again, I don't believe that the vast majority of people with disabilities, if given the option for integrated work, would select segregation.

The CHAIRMAN. All right. Thank you, Dr. Schroeder.

Jonathan Young, Dr. Young.

## STATEMENT OF JONATHAN YOUNG, Ph.D., CHAIR, NATIONAL COUNCIL ON DISABILITY, WASHINGTON, DC

Mr. YOUNG. First of all, Senator Harkin, thank you for convening this gathering, and thank you for your longstanding leadership for our community. As a Maryland resident, I also want to thank Senator Mikulski for her longstanding leadership.

There have been a lot of great points made, and I don't need to repeat my agreement with all of them. I'd like to try to focus on one theme, though, that I see emerging here, and it's a concept of bridging. Let me talk about this in a couple of respects.

As to the spectrum, as with all things, I start with the goals of the Americans with Disabilities Act, equality of opportunity, full participation, independent living, and economic self-sufficiency. What does that mean? That means that we want the same options, the same opportunities as all Americans without disabilities have.

Part of what we've been hearing in our work at the National Council on Disability is a huge gap between Federal policies and what's actually on the ground day-to-day. On one level it's simple to articulate policies. It's sometimes harder to get those policies translated down to the ground.

So there's a bridging piece that we need to figure out to close that gap. As you've heard from many people here today, we know what works. There are so many stories of where people have figured out creatively how to go about finding ways to meet their potential. Not everybody knows what works, though. People, Ms. Neas referenced returning veterans who have sustained new disabilities. They really need to figure out what works, and they're not necessarily engaged in the community that has all those paths laid out for them.

Since we know what works but not everybody knows how to make that work, the expectations, the attitudes do become so important. We can't micro-manage policies that directly get to that one-on-one collaboration for each individual, but the framework of expectations has such a profound impact.

There's a phrase that I like, "the dignity of risk." Ms. Petty referred earlier to dignity and respect. To me, when you talk about the dignity of risk, it means that every individual should have the opportunity to self-determine their own future, to have informed choices, the opportunity to make informed choices, to risk both having the chance to succeed but also the chance to fail. I don't mean to say that the goal at all is to fail, but there's something inherent in the opportunity to try, and we're not always going to be able to guarantee a successful outcome.

The other point that I want to mention as far as bridging is we have an inherited world, and we have a world that we want to become. We can't necessarily change the world instantly, but we need to find the strategies to get there.

One of the parts of the inherited world I think we struggle with is a focus on tasks, not skills. One of the things that I've heard repeatedly from employers is they're not looking for people that have been trained in a specific task. They're looking for people who have the skill sets to succeed on a job where they can help guide them to the kinds of tasks that need to be undertaken in a particular workplace.

I think part of the model we've inherited is, well, let's train an individual to do one specific task, as if that task is going to be viable for the next 50 years. That's not a great investment strategy.

We're better off investing in skills that are going to be adaptable to the environment as it changes.

Now, the other final point I'll make about bridging is your definition about people who need supports. There are economic aspects to that. There are costs associated with supports. So we need to figure out how to align resources, align the incentives in ways where resources we're dedicating to provide supports are most effectively aligned with effective self-determination and informed choice.

Maybe I'll just pause there.

The CHAIRMAN. Jonathan, you're saying that the theme that you kind of picked up here that kind of cuts through everything is the opportunity to make informed choices, the opportunity to advance, but also the opportunity to fail.

Now I'll say something maybe provocative to those who don't know this community very well, that sometimes I think people feel that someone with a disability, especially someone with an intellectual disability, we just can't permit them to ever fail. Why not? That's part of life. That's part of growing. I mean, sure, they may try something. Well, I've tried things in my life that I couldn't do either, that I failed at. So some of us are skilled in different ways. So what's wrong with building that kind of character to understand, well, OK, you tried that, it's not your deal; try something else. I think a lot of people that are not too much involved in the disability community don't understand that. I think somehow it's still perhaps part of what someone brought up here, a little bit of that pity, protectionism, have to take care of people, coddle, all that kind of stuff, so we can't permit people to fail like that, can permit people like me to fail but not people with significant disabilities.

Is that sort of what you're talking about?

Mr. YOUNG. Well, yes. And if I can follow up on that and perhaps use one story from my own personal experience as a graduate student in the history program at UNC-Chapel Hill, my first major writing seminar was with a Professor Peter Walker. He started out his first statement at the beginning of the seminar, and I can't convey his southern accent, sort of southern gentleman very slow presentation, but he told us every single one of you are going to fail this semester, and it took us all aback. We like to think that we're capable and competent people. And he kind of let that sit for a while for us to think about it. And he said, "the question is, can you have an elegant failure?"

[Laughter.]

His point was none of us were going to write a perfect paper, so just sort of get that out of the way. But let's focus now on, in the process, can you do an elegant job of failing that's going to show that you've advanced.

One of the things that we've talked about here thus far is expectations, and I think Dr. Schroeder referenced this, there's an assumption that people start out as being less than are deficient. I'd like to submit that in many respects, the people most equipped to succeed in our workplace are people with disabilities because each and every single day we have to develop strategies to adapt to a world that wasn't really set up for us.

The CHAIRMAN. Good point.

Mr. YOUNG. And I observe Dr. Schroeder here working with the microphone, with his name tag, and with a watch. I think of the ways that I navigate the world with my physical disability. There are things that we probably can't even put our fingers on, but there are aspects for individuals with disabilities and their families who are, from the moment of the disability, continually developing skills to think creatively about the world.

So like you said, we don't need to be guaranteed a chance to succeed. We do need to be guaranteed a chance to try, and if that means failing, many of the things that have been most helpful to me in my life have been where I failed. It hurt. It was awful. But I learned from it and went on to be better.

The CHAIRMAN. Sure. I think that's part of life's experiences.

I just see Ms. Neas has her sign up.

Ms. NEAS. I want to switch tactics just a little——

The CHAIRMAN. Oh, I'm sorry. Janet Samuelson. I'm sorry. Your name fell over, but you had your—I'm sorry, Ms. Neas. We'll come back to you.

Janet.

## STATEMENT OF JANET SAMUELSON, PRESIDENT AND CEO, SERVICESOURCE, ALEXANDRIA, VA

Ms. SAMUELSON. Senator Harkin, first and foremost, thank you so much for your advocacy on this important issue.

I think probably one of the reasons that I was invited here is not only because we serve people in a lot of different geographic areas and different geographic settings, urban and rural, but also we serve people with a lot of different types of services and different disabling conditions. Even when I go back to the definition that you provided way up front of someone with the most significant disability, there's a really pretty broad continuum of service needs and employment needs within that type of a definition.

I think that we all know that we don't have a comprehensive or holistic service delivery system for people, or funding system, support system through the Federal laws. As a service provider or broker between policy and Federal programs or State and local programs, we're working in some cases with WIA; we're working with the rehab act and the vocational rehabilitation systems; we're working with school systems and how transition plays out; we're working with local, State, and Federal resources that may be brought to the table; foundations; and in some cases charitable dollars.

But more importantly than anything else, I think if I look at the range of people that we serve, we operate services where we are the privatized vocational rehabilitation system in certain areas as a pilot project, all the way through day-habilitation, work or non-work activity type programs, that I probably serve people through our five organizations that represent every one of the viewpoints that you've heard here. So we have to be the integrator of understanding all of those perspectives and all of those ranges of needs.

When I look at the different funding systems and some of the ideas that you've heard here today, I think there are some very important things on the positive side. Senator Mikulski was talking about the changing labor force and how policy is still reacting to a previous design of labor. I think there are issues around assistive technology and access to technology and changed tools in the workplace, changed demands of the workplace.

There are a lot of opportunities for creative incentives. We're talking now to one of our State VR programs about looking at creating pathways for people from some of the contract employment opportunities directly into Federal employment.

I think there are a lot of good, positive things that can be done to move people with significant disabilities, by whatever your definition is, into the labor force and through the labor force, but I also think there's a little bit of a reality check that we need to think about when you're talking about policy versus implementation. You mentioned that with the recent recession and some of the downturn, that people with disabilities were exiting, not through their own choice, the labor market at 10 times the rate of other people.

I know from our experience, because we try to be very data-driven in looking at what we do, that we traditionally had been able to place, let's say, 1,200 to 1,500 people a year with community employers, with or without supports. That number, when the economy started tanking, got down as low as 500 people a year, less than half of the entry into the market for people, and that's, again, by whatever your definition of severe or significant disability is.

And so we have to deal with the realities of these various programs. We have to deal with the realities of resources that are available to support people and get them out. You have to deal with the realities from an employer standpoint of reasonable versus unreasonable accommodation and how you move that bar to a certain extent.

And again, when I look at all the numbers of people that we serve in my 30-plus years in the field, people have been able to—there's no question there are better opportunities available now than there have ever been. There's better understanding. There's a lot more implementation of good options for people, and certainly there is a lot more that we can be doing in those areas. But there are still people who, from a choice or developmental standpoint, have structural barriers to employment that don't allow them to enter the market in what would be considered a full and open, integrated, competitive employment definition.

I think it's so critical that we not negatively impact opportunities, we not restrict opportunities and create cliffs that mean that you have haves or have-nots.

My experience in working with the changed definition in the Rehabilitation Act program 10 years ago or so was that when you are in an environment—and so this isn't a slam at the VR system, because I think they're doing good work. But when you are in an environment where there are constrained resources, you don't have all the resources to serve people, and you have a definition that says people need to be able to achieve this, and what happens is that you end up having, with limited resources, people being served who can achieve certain outcomes, as opposed to over time develop to those outcomes.

I think in every one of our funding sources and our policy sources, it's important to be sure that we are finding ways within each of those to create and incent and develop new opportunities, as opposed to restrict opportunities while we develop, again, a broader continuum, a more organized continuum, and move people more and more toward the desirable goal, I believe, for every person with a disability, which is participation in the workforce.

The CHAIRMAN. Exactly. I just want to say, Ms. Samuelson, that I understand the realities of resources. I understand the realities of accommodations. Some of us, though, are trying to change those realities, the perceived realities. The perceived realities are that supportive services just simply cost a lot of money, and we don't have that money.

On the other hand, we seem to then say, "well, but OK, we'll do SSI and we'll do Medicaid, Title XIX," we'll do all those things, and that costs more money. But somehow we've got to change that reality of what resources are really most efficient.

But I know as a practitioner, someone like you who is out in the field every day, I know you have to deal with those realities. I'm just saying I hope that there are those of us—I see my good friend Senator Merkley is here. I know he is also interested in changing some of those realities, too, about how do we deal with these resources so that the resources we have are focused more on providing the opportunity to make informed choices, the opportunity to have early intervention programs, because we know those are the most cost-effective if you just look at it from a budgetary standpoint, a resource standpoint.

Ms. SAMUELSON. I was just going to say to that point exactly, when you see restrictions in services, as you found in the rehab act, what happens is people that might have been served through that funding stream being shifted into Medicaid waiver programs, where the services are more expensive and the design is not oriented toward work, permissible work in the same way.

The CHAIRMAN. Absolutely.

Now I'm going to recognize Ms. Neas.

Or, Senator Merkley, would you like to interject something here right now? I'll recognize Senator Merkley, who is, again, a very valuable member of this committee and was also a very valued member of the Oregon legislature, where he was the leader and I know he's worked on these issues for a long time.

Senator Merkley.

## STATEMENT OF SENATOR MERKLEY

Senator MERKLEY. Thank you, Mr. Chair.

I really just want to thank you all for coming. This underlying issue of how you provide work and employment opportunities that both provide financial resources and an appropriate workplace is very important, for all workers, whether they have disabilities or not. A job is something that not only provides finances, but it feeds the soul. And so trying to wrestle with the best possible way that we can create a framework for that employment is a very important issue. On my team, we've been talking to folks about trying to understand the pros and cons of different approaches, and hearing your thoughts here is very useful. Thank you for coming and wrestling with it.

The CHAIRMAN. Thank you very much, Senator Merkley.

Ms. Neas, you're next. Then I'll recognize Mr. Pearson.

Ms. NEAS. I want to just add two concepts that have been raised. One is this whole notion of assistive technology. We are seeing, particularly in an education environment, that kids that we thought had very limited cognitive abilities, when they're given the right adaptive equipment, are able to demonstrate that they don't have significantly different cognitive abilities. I think we need to make sure that people who need certain devices and supports get them, and that that can be life transforming.

I think of our friend Bob Williams. When I first met him, he had a laminated board that he pointed to, and now he's got this very groovy electronic talking liberator that makes communicating with him a lot easier. I think about if Bob had to do what Fred was talking about, working in a mattress factory, that wouldn't work so well for him as a person with significant cerebral palsy.

I think being able to give people the tools they need to do what they can do is something that's really important.

And then the other component I think is support employment is something that's just grossly under-funded, and we really need to be able to give people those ongoing, not time-limited but ongoing, on-the-job supports, that people may need different levels during the course of whatever it is they're doing, but that concept of ongoing, long-term supports for people to be in the community working is something that we're just desperate for.

The CHAIRMAN. Technology, you're right. I'm glad you mentioned Bob Williams because he's one of the most fantastic writers I've ever met.

Ms. NEAS. Exactly.

The CHAIRMAN. Just a beautiful writer. But with severe cerebral palsy, it would always hold him back. Now, through technology, he can let that ability that he has, which is incredible——

Ms. NEAS. And having a conversation with him before this device required a great deal of determination to pay attention to each word and to be able to remember 20 words ago to get to the end of the sentence what he was saying, which you could do, but it required a great deal of concentration beyond a typical conversation. And so to have him now be able to just communicate directly is a much more effective way.

The CHAIRMAN. Incorporating technology is very important.

Let's see. Mr. Pearson, you had your——

Mr. PEARSON. I just wanted to make two brief points, and it's in line with supportive technologies.

In manufacturing, we consistently improve the process. And just as freedoms that African-Americans sought made everybody else freer, in the manufacturing process, when you begin to improve the process, it improves everyone else's productivity.

The CHAIRMAN. Sure.

Mr. PEARSON. So that's what's gained when we begin to think outside the box.

And the other point we talked about earlier is failure. Well, if you compare—an employer should always compare, and this is not anecdotal data on my part, it's actual. We've been more successful with retention with our employees who have been disabled, and it went back to that earlier point of loyalty. Turnover is expensive. What is less expensive is retention. And by focusing on that group of loyal employees and investing in recruiting, and what is minimal expenses in terms of accommodation, which is often viewed as a dirty word, is actually in most instances very inexpensive and goes back to my first point of everyone begins to share in a productivity improvement.

The CHAIRMAN. Sure.

Now, I'm going to recognize some people. Everybody's got their cards up. But remember when I started this discussion, there were two things I wanted to hopefully bring out in this roundtable discussion. One was sort of the spectrum of opportunities, the spectrum of getting people into employment. But the other aspect was career enhancement.

It's one thing to get into a job. The other thing is how do we build systems so that people can advance in a career, people with significant disabilities, how they can get a job, training, opportunities for advancement. How do we work that in? So that you don't just say, "OK, we got you a job, and that's what you're going to do the rest of your life." Well, sometimes people like to try different things, advance, do different things. What do we need to do to sort of help the private sector integrated employment so that they have career opportunities and advancement?

I want you to think about that, and if we can bring that up. Ms. Moore, you had yours up. Then I'll go to Ms. Petty, Ms. Pumphrey, Mr. Schroeder, from left to right, and then Mr. Young.

OK, Ms. Moore.

Ms. MOORE. Well, I'd like to go back to what Mr. Young said about bridging. I think as we look at a more complete implementation of what we actually know how to do in our field to include everyone, if we say "all means all," that's not just an ideological perspective. It's really a commitment.

A piece of that is to say, "all right, you brought up voc rehab, what we measure is what we produce." So what is it that we're giving guidance to? What are we enforcing? What are we measuring? What are the performance outcomes that we actually expected? Have we set some targeted goals? You talked about the huge discrepancy, Senator, between the unemployment rates right now for people who are not perceived to have disabilities and for people who do, and it's huge. And in order to shift that, we do have to commit to certain things and begin to divest from other things.

I would suggest that if we are going to move away from segregation in a skillful, planful way, we need to commit to that in measureable ways, planful ways, and we need to have clear, supportive leadership. We have national policies. We have laws. We have people's protections under the law in terms of the ADA, the voc rehab act, under Olmstead, as people have suggested, but it's not aspirational. This is actually the policy of the United States.

On the ground where we're doing that, we need to hold people to it, and I think we have some really good examples. Nobody is perfect. No system is perfect. We're imperfect people. But if you look to places like Vermont or Washington State, where there was sustained leadership with a very clear policy, a very clear set of measures of what are we moving toward, and consensus building among all the partners, including people running sheltered workshops to say we're going to move toward more customized supported employment, real jobs, integrated work, meaningful wages, and we are going to move away from some other models. They didn't dump people in the street, but now they have roughly twice the positive employment outcomes of other States because they made that commitment.

There was never a question about a little of this, a little of that. I mean, one of the reasons we had the Olmstead decision is because States were a little confused about the ADA. They thought, all things being equal, a little segregation, a little integration, great, and that actually wasn't the law.

We have the same thing in employment.

The CHAIRMAN. That's right.

OK, I'm going to go to Ms. Petty, but then I want to skip to Jonathan Young down at the end to talk about policies that we need to put in place to increase earnings and advancement in the workforce.

I'm going to start with Ms. Petty.

Ms. PETTY. I wanted to go back and talk a little bit about the resources. And I did not understand because I see many, many hundreds of people working in segregated employment, and that works out to get these huge contracts, and all that money going into the workshops, I think, can be used to help people have a job with dignity.

I live in the Wal-Mart capital of the world.

The CHAIRMAN. That's right. The chicken capital also.

Ms. PETTY. I know that Wal-Mart contracts with some of the sheltered workshops in our area, and we just want the employers to change their attitude, as I said earlier. It's about attitude and thinking that everybody can have a job. So I think we need to start there, and I wanted to address your career question.

I think it starts in one area with voc rehab. When I was going to school, I did not see my vocational rehab counselor. I didn't even know what that was, so I didn't see them until I was a senior in high school. And I think we need to start earlier.

I have two little boys, and people already ask them what do you want to be when you grow up. I think we need to start earlier, and you've been talking about the early intervention. And so that might be able to help shape policy if we can start working kids earlier and helping them. And, you know, I went to college, and I changed my major a few times. I really didn't know what I wanted to be even when I was out of high school.

Thank you, and that's all I have.

The CHAIRMAN. All right. Thanks, Ms. Petty.

Jon, OK. I'll just change the focus a little bit here on career. I think Ms. Petty just kind of put her finger on it there. She didn't see voc rehab much. Hopefully we're going to try to change that. But getting people to think about careers and how they advance, and how do we make sure that people with disabilities don't just get—it's OK to get a job, but how about career advancement?

Mr. YOUNG. Thank you, and I think it's a great point that you start with there, because there may be a tendency to think of a job as a static moment as opposed to a person's life. There's a phrase that "people are policy." I think when we look at the lives that we see people living, it's an expression of our policies. To have policies that are effective, they need to be attuned to an entire person's life.

Let me come back to two points. I used the expression "dignity of risk." There's a discussion about reality. I think we do need to recognize that not everybody has the same risk threshold, if you will, in terms of how much risk they're willing to take. So as we look at policy changes, we need to be mindful of the—informed choice means an informed choice about the risks given today's environment, and that includes an environment of very difficult economic circumstances.

As we talk about the difficult economic circumstances, though, we've got to be mindful that the costs also are not static. I think we often tend to look at costs in one area and say, "oh, well, that's too expensive," and you hinted at this earlier. But by not investing in people in certain respects, we're risking raising costs significantly otherwise.

We spent billions of dollars on education programs for people with disabilities. If the endpoint of those education programs is a lifetime of entitlements without providing as much opportunity as possible for people to live independently in communities of their choosing, to be engaged and earn as much as they can in the setting of their choosing, our economics are backward.

We need to recognize limited resources, but we can't focus narrowly on certain investment of costs without paying attention to what the opportunity costs, if you will, are by not investing in those. In terms of the policies that we need to undertake, to me the core piece becomes incentives, and a few people have talked about this. We need to focus on where we establish policies and where we invest resources, what incentives does that create.

You mentioned earlier—a few people have mentioned the role of internships. I'm proud to say that I had no idea what I wanted to do in high school and was really a pretty awful student. I was a wrestler. When I went to college I was going to be an engineer because math was the easiest thing for me, and then I worked for Congressman Tony Coelho for a semester after my freshman year in college, and I'm here today, among other reasons, because Tony Coelho had me sit in the majority whip office and attend majority meetings, and I got bitten by the bug of politics.

A lot of people with disabilities, if you're living on certain benefits, that prohibits certain amounts of income. There are many people that go through school and don't get the chance to have those internships because doing that means they lose certain things, and those economic resources are important and valuable.

And if those incentives are aligned away from participation, that has a cascading effect, because missing that internship at one point or missing the opportunities throughout the early periods of schooling are going to make it harder to have sequential job development.

I know I'm being fairly high-level here, but I think if we could focus on incentives and figure out where the resources are that we have to invest because we're going to pay for it if we don't, but let's invest those resources where the incentives are aligned with the goals that we all know and agree on, enshrined in the ADA.

The CHAIRMAN. Very good. Thank you.

Mr. Schroeder, I'm going to call on you, Fred, in just a second here, and then Ms. Pumphrey. But before I do, we've been joined by Senator Franken, and again, someone who is a great member of this committee, and also someone who I know is committed to the goals of the ADA and making sure that we have the resources that we need, and that we invest those resources wisely.

Senator Franken, welcome. Thank you for being here, and I'll recognize you for comments or questions.

### STATEMENT OF SENATOR FRANKEN

Senator FRANKEN. I apologize for getting here late. I was stuck in a Judiciary Executive Committee where we needed to keep a quorum.

But this is our second hearing on this, and I have just one basic question. I've been to a sheltered workshop situation where there seemed to be people working who were severely disabled and who were really having a good time, I mean really happy in the work. And then we had a hearing here, and we had a gentleman who was pretty severely disabled who actually was in an integrated work environment and spoke incredibly highly of it. I don't know if you remember, but this is like the biggest laugh that we've ever gotten since I've been here. He had Down syndrome, and I asked, I said, "why do you enjoy it?," and he said, he likes joking around with his supervisor. And I said, "does your supervisor have a good sense of humor?" And he said, he took a pause and he went, "Is this on the record?"

[Laughter.]

And he knew exactly what he was doing. So as a former comedy writer and comedian, I consider a sense of humor to be maybe the highest form of intelligence.

[Laughter.]

This may have been, in a way, the most intelligent person ever to testify in my experience thus far.

But my question really is—and I understand the Vermont example of segueing from a sheltered workshop setting much more toward integrated. My question really is, is there a place for sheltered workshops, and are sheltered workshops a better place, or do you distinguish between severity and nature of the disability when considering whether there is a place for sheltered workshops? That's for anyone.

Ms. MOORE. I don't know if Fred wants to take that.

The CHAIRMAN. Do we need the question repeated, or do you understand it?

Ms. MOORE. I'll do it if you want.

The CHAIRMAN. All right. Ms. Moore, you're first up.

Ms. MOORE. Well, I think to both address the question of how do we best advance people's careers and to answer the question of to what extent does level or type of disability possibly predispose people to be seen as more appropriate for sheltered work, I think sheltered workshops have a place because they're here and because we have so many, hundreds of thousands of people in sheltered workshops. So no matter what we decide here, there will be a role for sheltered workshops as we move forward.

I think that relative to the level, type of disability, we've really gone way beyond that in terms of our ability to look at a person, and until we can do this we'll never be able to figure out the advancement of the career either, because we're really looking at the contribution the person can make and then saying what's the negotiated relationship with the——

Senator FRANKEN. Are you saying there's sort of a danger, when talking about level of disability, of basically categorizing people and not looking at everyone's individual capacities?

Ms. MOORE. Absolutely. I know one of the first people I ever got a job for was somebody who had long-term institutionalization, was deaf and blind, and had developmental and cognitive disabilities, and she was just not considered employable based on how she looked in that environment, her lack of experience, her lack of frame of reference, and people weren't able to figure out how to communicate with her right away.

We did a fairly extensive process of coming to really try lots of things, to what Ms. Neas said, and what we discovered was there were things that just really did light her up. And not surprisingly, given her dual sensory impairment, she really liked manipulating things, putting things together. We ended up—now, that could have—arguably, people could have said, "oh, she likes putting things together, let's send her to a sheltered workshop. She has significant multiple disabilities."

But we ended up getting her a job at American Electric Wire and Cable, building computer cable harnesses that it turns out you can do—we taught her. By the way, we structured the environment, did hand over hand. We used systematic instruction and the assistive technology. That was back in the 1980s, so we've advanced way beyond that now. But we had to picture her making a contribution and recognize there was absolutely nothing that we could provide for her in a segregated setting that couldn't be provided where that work usually occurs.

I understand that it's not a simple thing to move from where we've been to where we're going, but I think we have learned a lot not just about skills but we've also learned that people can make a contribution that is not just specific to skills, and I think those of us who have been employers recognize that.

The CHAIRMAN. I hate to jump around here, but Mr. Schroeder has been trying to get in here for a long time.

Did you want to address yourself to this specific question that Senator Franken raised, or was there something else, Fred?

Mr. SCHROEDER. Well, actually, I think it's a good segue into the whole question about upward mobility, that if a person is placed in a facility that has a very limited range of activities, the idea that the person would have a maximum or even a reasonable opportunity to prepare for upward mobility I think is questionable.

We issued a rule when I was with the Rehabilitation Services Administration back in 2001 that ended the practice of people being placed in sheltered work through the Vocational Rehabilitation Program. And the reason we did it is because the essence of public policy, as Jonathan was talking about a few minutes ago, is aligning your incentives around the activity that you want to increase, and we believed that sheltered work did not afford people not only the level of employment that we believe people could attain given the right supports and training, but specifically the upward mobility.

Just not to belabor numbers, but one of the things we looked at was whether people who were employed in sheltered work, in fact, developed skills that enabled them to leave the facility and move into integrated work, and our data showed that fewer than 1 percent left sheltered employment each year for integrated employment. And so the incentive we felt was not there.

And if you look at the broader incentive system, there are hundreds of millions of dollars of noncompetitive Federal contracts, as well as other types of contracts, that go to facilities, but there's no particular incentive to maximize the individual's earnings, there's no incentive built in to move the person into higher-level employment, there's no incentive even to have the work be sufficient to be reasonably self-sustaining; in other words, the hours of work.

If we think about work at its most basic level, there are people who do volunteer work, of course, but by and large we equate work with earning enough money to be self-sustaining, and our data did not see, certainly didn't reflect that sheltered work was achieving that end. We wanted to press the system toward integrated work that paid a competitive wage, that was challenging and interesting to the individual on the assumption that that's the best platform for people to advance in employment.

The CHAIRMAN. Dr. Schroeder, thank you very much.

Now, let's see, I'm trying to figure out who to go to next. Ms. Petty, OK, go ahead.

Ms. PETTY. I wanted to answer Senator Franken. You said that the person you met, he liked the sheltered workshop. Is that right?

Senator FRANKEN. I'm sorry. The person I met where?

Ms. PETTY. He liked to be in the sheltered workshop? He enjoyed it?

Senator FRANKEN. The person who testified here?

Ms. PETTY. No. You said you went to a sheltered workshop, and they were happy, right?

Senator FRANKEN. Oh, right, right. Yeah.

Ms. PETTY. Well, my question would be what was it that made them happy at the sheltered workshop, and why wouldn't they be able to be happy in the community? Because if I remember right, we ended segregation many, many years ago. So people with disabilities, especially intellectual disabilities, is a form of segregation, and that is not our civil rights. That goes against our civil rights.

I just wanted to say that. Thank you.

Senator FRANKEN. I think that's a great question. I mean, my observation was that there are people, a number of people seem severely cognitively disabled, and that they were really having a good time, I mean really enjoying their experience, like laughing a lot. I mean, it was an extremely happy environment.

It made me feel that the people who had provided or who had put this together were doing a really good thing, and my question really was that from my really brief experience there, that I would say that there was a difference in the level of disability between the young man who testified who got that huge laugh and the people that were there. He was working for Hewlett Packard, and he seemed to be an extremely intelligent, capable guy from every metric that I could think of, other than the fact that he had Down syndrome, but he was really smart.

On the other hand, I'm not certainly an expert in this, and that's what I was really asking. I'm asking from a standpoint of real ignorance on my part, and humility. But I'm wondering—just take my question at face value. And your answer is why wouldn't they be happy also in an integrated situation, and they probably would be. I think these people, the particular people I'm thinking of, there were two who sat next to each other who seemed to be laughing a tremendous amount at each other's jokes and were having a much better time at their work than most people have a right to.

[Laughter.]

That was my experience.

The CHAIRMAN. They were having a better time than we usually have here is what you're saying.

Senator FRANKEN. This committee is incredibly enjoyable, Mr. Chairman.

[Laughter.]

The CHAIRMAN. Ms. Pumphrey, could you respond to this? Because you have a son with very severe and significant disabilities. You spoke about that earlier. What's your observation on this?

Ms. PUMPHREY. I still maintain that there's a point or a place in this society for sheltered workshops. That's where my son is, and I believe that that option needs to be there for individuals with significant disabilities.

One of the things I would like to see happen to help with the cost of the services of placing individuals with significant disabilities in the community is the Consumer Choice Options program through the Intellectual Disabilities Waiver allows me to manage his services at a significantly reduced cost than if I were purchasing his services through an agency. If I were able to purchase through the Consumer Choice Option program the supportive employment piece, I could do that very cheaply and allow him to work in the community doing the work that he enjoys. Unfortunately, the way that the waiver is designed, that's not an option at this time.

I would really like to see the Consumer Choice Options piece of the waiver, those guidelines opened up some.

The CHAIRMAN. OK.

Ms. Samuelson.

Ms. SAMUELSON. To answer Senator Franken's question and segue it back to your question, which I know you're trying to get answered, the second one, and I think also to tie into Dr. Young's point, if you're trying to look to the future and how to move where you want to go from a public policy standpoint, then you have to start with people and systems where they are and figure out how you can make things change.

If you have people who are served in a segregated or a work center environment, and we do, we have three work center programs in three of the States that we operate, a very small percentage of the total number of people that we serve, but that's where people are. That's either where they've ended up, or sometimes it serves as a safety net for people who have been out, and then as their needs change and they're less able to work, they come back in.

Then how do you begin to develop the incentives and systems to support moving the bar or creating opportunities without, again, creating a service cliff that eliminates opportunities for people because they can't qualify or there aren't enough resources in the system at the current time to take them where they need to be?

And to Dr. Schroeder's point about the changed definition and placement, what we found was that people who might have gotten into the vocational rehabilitation system and been served with a broader definition, and then for continuing types of services in an environment of limited resources instead don't get into those systems. A very small fraction of the people that we serve in employment programs, by our definition of people who have most significant disabilities, are people who have entered through the vocational rehabilitation system, and that's not the way that you want it to be if that's meant to be our primary service driving program to support not only the initial employment but also the career development for people with disabilities.

And to the point of what do you do when you have somebody who is in a less-than-ideal from full inclusion and full opportunity employment, I think that there are many proven strategies that can be incented into the systems. I know we do a lot of what in the workforce investment system would be called incumbent worker retraining, to help encourage people to broaden their career interests and move through systems. You've got assessments, you've got mentorship programs, you've got internships.

You've got a lot of ways to expose people to alternate skill and work environments, but you also need to have ways to do supported transitions when it's a question of risk management and how much somebody is willing to try, and that can include some strategies that we've tried, like guaranteeing service slots for people that are willing to try different things but still come back, and transportation, which is a huge issue for people in terms of work environments, and it's a huge issue—I know we're not talking about Social Security, but it's a complex issue because there's the whole overlay in terms of all of the programs and supports that come through some of the entitlement programs, SSI and SSDI.

I think if we focus on incentives and the things that we know about what works and how to build those into our delivery systems without restricting options for people, then we can start with people where they are and help them find new opportunities.

The CHAIRMAN. Exactly.

Ms. Neas.

Ms. NEAS. Senator, I think the two concepts that are really important here, one is informed choice. Did anybody ever ask him, what do you want to do?

Senator FRANKEN. I don't know.

Ms. NEAS. And that's a factor.

The other is how risk averse or how much are people willing to take a risk? My experience is the older people are, sometimes the less willing we are to take a risk, and if this works for me, then it works for me and please don't change it.

I think we want to have particularly kids coming out of school thinking that they have more choices than just one option. On the other hand, I think we don't want to take away a place for people to earn some income and replace it with nothing if nothing is the other option.

The CHAIRMAN. Anyone else wanted to add something to this or expound on something? Jonathan? You looked like you were ready to jump in there on this.

Mr. YOUNG. I was thinking about it, but now I have to move from thinking to talking.

Let me try to make two brief points, one I think we need to hold out as an ultimate measure of quality of life. I think what becomes challenging, then, is determining how do we measure quality of life, and who measures quality of life, and to return to earlier themes, ultimately I think each individual needs to measure their own quality of life.

To measure one's own quality of life, there also needs to be sufficient awareness of what life opportunities and options there are. But let me come up on the theme a moment ago about starting where people are. I'm a pragmatist by philosophical bent, and so I've always wanted to do things from the ground up. I think that's a powerful point to begin with.

Whatever we may say about how things are or are not working, there's a moment that we're at right now. There are people who are living right now in certain experiences, which include certain segregated settings, as well as integrated settings, and I think we need to start from the vantage point of people's individual lives, what is working or may not be working, and what more they might learn or what might be made available to them that could move from a particular place to another place, including people where the opportunity that they're in might be satisfactory for the moment but there's a clear development issue.

If I'm 25 years old and in an entry-level job of some kind, that's not the end of the story. I mean, you want to look at development opportunities. At all points of the life spectrum, whether we're in school or at any point in the employment spectrum, the dialogue I think needs to begin with trying to assess the quality of life where one is, and how do we identify particular strategies that move an individual to a place of their choosing of greater opportunity.

The CHAIRMAN. Got it.

Dr. Schroeder.

Mr. SCHROEDER. Very briefly, going back to the idea of incentives, and also the public's conception of disability, I'd just like to say very clearly that I believe that the sub-minimum wage system needs to end, and I say that knowing all of the counter arguments. But we live in a society that assumes that people with disabilities are less productive, and therefore the sub-minimum wage system I think perpetuates that viewpoint.

Second, the sub-minimum wage system removes any incentive to try to find a better match for the individual. It is a premise that given the person's disability, he or she will be less productive, and that assumption then is passed on to the individual in terms of a sub-minimum wage.

And so I think one very clear thing that would advance the employment of people with disabilities is to eliminate Section 14(c) of the Fair Labor Standards Act, and that presses our entire system to explore employment opportunities that are really capitalizing on the inherent abilities of the people with whom we work.

The CHAIRMAN. Mr. Pearson. And this may be the last comment because our time has run out. Go ahead, Mr. Pearson.

Mr. PEARSON. With that, Senator, there is no substitute for a solid human resources policy and integration in the workforce. If you want people to advance, they have to be evaluated, those records have to be reviewed, and then opportunities increased for people with disabilities, because employers will invest in folks who are loyal. They'll invest in people who have a demonstrated work history of performance, and integration is key to getting that done.

The CHAIRMAN. I agree.

Did you have something you wanted to add?

Senator FRANKEN. No. Thank you all.

The CHAIRMAN. It's a great discussion.

Senator FRANKEN. And thank you for addressing my very basic question. Thank you.

The CHAIRMAN. Thank you all very much. I think this has been a rich discussion, a great roundtable.

I'll make a couple of observations in closing. Since I'm the chair, I get a closing. I have the gavel, as they say.

I think we touched on some important policy issues, how we make competitive integrated employment available to all, even people with the most significant disabilities. We touched briefly, of course, on the whole issue of 14(c), the sub-minimum wage issue. It seems to me that the idea of sheltered workshops, when it was started, was really cutting edge. It was getting people out of homes, out of institutions and into workplaces, where they could associate with people, learn skill sets, do things. It was wonderful. It was really cutting edge.

Of course, I think we've advanced. There were a lot of things that were cutting edge back sometime, but maybe now we've moved. Society moves. And so just the whole verbiage of sheltered workshop, I don't like that. For some reason, it just gnaws at me. I like the idea of work centers, that type of thing. But the idea of a sheltered workshop? We've moved beyond that, Jonathan. We're moving beyond that concept.

The question really, I think, for us is, as I think someone pointed out, I forget who it was, we have hundreds of thousands of people now working in these work centers. I'm not going to call them— I'm going to get rid of that language out of my lexicon here. These work centers that are there, we have to recognize the reality of that. But how do we start moving? It's just like with the ADA. I mean, we knew we couldn't change everything overnight. It takes years, and sometimes you have setbacks, like U.S. Supreme Court decisions, and then you work to overcome those. But it's a steady progress.

How do we now, equipped with more knowledge, better technology, understanding the economics of the realities—I mean, we know, we have studies that show that—it was a 2011 study I have here in front of me from Kent State University that showed that the cost of supportive employment was 40 percent less than those in work centers or sheltered workshops. So we know that there's some cost effectiveness there.

However, having said that, I think what we're trying to move toward is where there will be early integration, early programs, early intervention programs where young kids with significant disabilities are challenged, where they are provided opportunities for internships to see where their skill sets might lie, and the assumption should be that everyone can be in integrated employment. That should be the basic assumption, and our goals ought to be moving in that direction, and that's what we're trying to do, is move in that direction, recognizing, as I said, the reality that there are hundreds of thousands of people in work centers right now, and whoever said that, you might take more risk when you're younger, but when you're 35 or 40 or 45, and this is what I've been doing, and I know how to do this, and I feel comfortable there, and I may be happy there, do we uproot all that? Do we uproot that? I mean, who am I to try to uproot that?

But it seems to me that we need to make that transition from the cutting edge of what these workshops were in the beginning now to a new cutting edge, a cutting edge of integrated employment and the future for young people in that setting. I recognize you can't do it overnight, but we ought to at least be moving in that direction.

While I understand—believe me, nothing upsets me more than sub-minimum wage. There was this situation in Iowa that really triggered my thinking in this and said, "wait a minute, this is an old concept. We've got to get rid of this." And what was happening there finally brought me to this realization that there has to be a new regime, a new way of doing things here.

As I said, it's been a rich discussion. Do I have all the answers right now? I don't. I don't pretend to have all the answers. But I do believe there's a general consensus, I think among all the disability groups, that we do want to move more toward fully integrated employment to the maximum extent possible, and then recognize that for many, many, many Americans, their work in the work centers that they've been doing for many years, that maybe as we move ahead we can't just disrupt lives inordinately overnight. But we at least have to start with young people now and give them a new cutting edge.

That's why I appreciated the opportunity here. I look forward to continued discussions, input from all of you and from the entire community as we move ahead on this. We'll feel our way forward. But again, I hope you'll look at what we're trying to do in the WIA bill, the Workforce Investment Act, to start to move in this direction, where the default setting is integrated employment, where the assumption is kids will be trained by VR and working early on to give them these skill sets, and I've learned a lot here just in terms of options—internships and opportunities so people can try different things. That's got to be part of this also, I think, for voc rehab.

We're feeling our way forward. But I think we are moving forward, and I continue to ask for your input in that.

We'll leave the record open for 10 days. Participants may submit statements or supplements for the record. That includes all of you or any Senators who were here or couldn't come because of other committee assignments.

And with that, unless there's something else to be said, the committee will stand adjourned.

Thank you very much, all of you.

[Additional material follows.]

## ADDITIONAL MATERIAL

PREPARED STATEMENT OF ADVANCING EMPLOYMENT CONNECTING PEOPLE (APSE)

Chairman Harkin, Chairman Enzi and members of the committee, thank you for the opportunity to submit testimony related to the roundtable.

APSE is a national non-profit membership organization, founded in 1988 as the Association for Persons in Supported Employment, now known as APSE. APSE is the *only* national organization with an *exclusive focus* on integrated employment and career advancement opportunities for individuals with disabilities. APSE has chapters in 35 States and the District of Columbia. Our members come from all 50 States and Puerto Rico, as well as several foreign countries.

The evidence is extremely clear: people with intellectual and developmental disabilities can successfully work in the community. For over 20 years, the Institute for Community Inclusion has tracked employment outcomes for individuals served by State developmental disability agencies. According to the most recently available data, 20.3 percent of individuals are served in integrated employment—i.e., jobs in the community. After peaking at 25 percent in 2001, this figure has remained flat since 2004.

This is unacceptable, particularly as you look more closely at this data and see the massive variation among States. Washington State leads the Nation at 88 percent, with Oklahoma at 60 percent. Vermont, Maryland, Louisiana, New Hampshire, and New Mexico are also States that are well above the national average. This is a highly diverse group of States, which have proven quite clearly that we can do a lot better than a 20 percent rate of individuals working in the community.

So what makes the difference? For starters, it requires a clear vision and commitment to community employment by State leadership, followed by specific actions that act on this vision. It also requires within that vision, a culture that employment in the community is a natural and expected outcome. Absolutely critical is for States to use their resources, primarily funded by Medicaid, to provide incentives for and support services that are in line with that vision, and to also limit or deny funding for service alternatives such as facility-based services. It also requires a comprehensive approach in terms of addressing all the various aspects of operating a service system to ensure that the vision of community employment is supported. This includes ongoing staff development, with both systems staff and service providers, so that they not only embrace this vision, but also have the technical knowledge to implement it.

It also requires addressing a wide range of other issues: service monitoring and quality assurance, engagement of individuals and families, the availability of benefits counseling that supports community employment, transportation, inter-agency collaboration with public vocational rehabilitation, to name just a few. Strong transition services from school-to-work, with a clear focus on community employment are also critical. One area that we have found that is absolutely vital is the need for a strong data measurement and monitoring system. It is clear that those States that are closely monitoring data regarding performance in community employment consistently achieve better outcomes, proving that old truism "You manage what you measure."

We would urge the Federal Government to require States to have comprehensive employment data measurement systems for integrated community employment. This could be accomplished via the authority of CMS, which provides the vast majority of resources to State intellectual and developmental disability agencies. Along with all of these other factors, I should also add that moving forward on community employment can take significant political will. Many States have well-funded and politically connected entities, consisting primarily of service providers interested in maintaining the status quo.

Leaders of State intellectual and developmental disability agencies must be provided the support to stand up to these interests that are odds with the public policies of the United States that via the ADA, Olmstead Decision, IDEA, etc. that clearly state that disability is a natural part of human experience that in no way diminishes a person's right to fully participate in all aspects of life—including employment alongside their fellow non-disabled citizens. It is not acceptable to use public resources in a way that is in conflict with our national disability policy.

PREPARED STATEMENT OF THE NATIONAL DISABILITY RIGHTS NETWORK (NDRN)

THE NEED FOR NEW STRATEGIES FOR IMPROVING EMPLOYMENT FOR PEOPLE WITH
DISABILITIES

As the nonprofit membership organization for the federally mandated Protection and Advocacy Systems and Client Assistance Programs for people with disabilities, the National Disability Rights Network (NDRN) would like to thank Senators Harkin and Enzi and the Senate Committee on Health, Education, Labor, and Pensions, for their recent attention to the employment-related needs of people with disabilities. This hearing and the July 14, 2011, hearing on Strategies for Improving Employment for People with Disabilities, as well as the March 2, 2011, hearing on Employment Opportunities for People with Disabilities, demonstrate a continued commitment to improving the employment situation for people with disabilities.

People with disabilities continue to face unemployment at a rate much higher than that of the general population. According to the Office of Disability Employment Programs, the unemployment rate for people with disabilities in June 2011 was 16.9 percent, compared with 9.0 percent for persons with no disability. Moreover, over 78 percent of the non-institutional population with disabilities ages 16 years and over is not in the labor force at all, meaning that they may have given up on seeking employment or not be aware of employment services available.[1]

Many individuals with disabilities are working in segregated settings for subminimum wage. In its January 2011 report, *Segregated & Exploited: A Call to Action!*, NDRN documented the risks of exploitation and abuse that come with segregated or subminimum wage settings, and discussed case studies of people with disabilities paid extremely low wages for years, with little review of the role that vocational rehabilitation agencies are intended to play in providing services for people to leave segregated workshops or subminimum wage positions. Also, there is little monitoring of the requirement that education agencies take into account each student's preferences or interests when transitioning people with disabilities from education into the workplace, or that vocational rehabilitation agencies have a role in this transition. The report is available at *http://www.ndrn.org/images/ Documents/ Resources/Publications/Reports/Segregated-and-Exploited.pdf*.

Segregated employment and work at subminimum wages limit the ability of people with disabilities to become independent, self-sufficient members of the community. Almost all employment options within segregated workshops are unskilled, low-wage jobs with few, if any, benefits, and few opportunities for advancement. Consistent isolation of people with disabilities from people without disabilities can hinder the proper development of socialization skills and self-esteem. As the disability community has long understood, integration leads to increased satisfaction with their living and working arrangements and increased overall happiness, as well as improved adaptive behavior skills. Segregated workshops provide little, if any, benefit for people with disabilities, and the Federal Government should end Medicaid and other Federal funding of these programs.

NDRN supports the increased use of supported and customized employment as a way to enhance the ability of people with disabilities to work in an integrated and competitive setting, based on an "employment first" model. In such a model, vocational rehabilitation agencies and education officials working on transitioning of people with disabilities into employment focus first on finding the person an appropriate job, and then finding the services and supports necessary to make that employment a reality. Customized employment means individualizing the relationship between employees and employers in a way that meets the needs of both, based both on the strengths and interests of the employee and on the needs of the employer. A customized job may differ from the employer's standard job descriptions, but is based on actual tasks that are found in the workplace and meet the unmet needs of the employer. It may include employment through job carving, self-employment, or entrepreneurial initiatives.

Examples of the successful use of customized employment services to successfully provide competitive employment to people with disabilities, at competitive wages, exist throughout the country. The Georgia Advocacy Office (the Georgia Protection and Advocacy agency) has worked with vocational rehabilitation agencies and employers to develop demonstrations of successful customized employment for people with disabilities. The State of Washington has also developed a supported employment program, and has established customized employment services as the primary use of day program and employment funds within the State.

---

[1] "Economic News Release," Bureau of Labor Statistics, June 2011, *available at* <http:// www.bls.gov/news.release/empsit.t06.htm>.

The Federal Government should, based on these and other examples, enact policies that support and encourage the spread of customized employment. Congress should work with the Department of Labor to ensure that vocational rehabilitation agencies have an active role in providing customized employment services to people with disabilities. Specifically, the term "most significant disabilities" should be federally defined and monitored to ensure that vocational rehabilitation agencies provide priority services to people with the most significant disabilities first, as required by law. The Federal Schedule A program should also be a tool to provide customized employment for people with disabilities, with some changes to better implement the program in a way that supports customized employment.

Although Theodore Roosevelt proclaimed in his State of the Union Address on December 3, 1907, that "the National government should be a model employer," Federal employment of people with disabilities continues to decline. Executive orders and goals are helpful, but are more effective if there are specific mandates and Federal agencies are held responsible for complying with directives. Statistics from the Equal Employment Opportunity Commission (EEOC) show that individuals with a disability in the Federal Government come into employment at a lower grade than non-disabled peers and experience little career advancement. Hiring and supervisory staff must understand the capabilities of each person with a disability and offer a full range of mentoring opportunities and support in order to assure career growth and advancement.

NDRN is happy to continue working with the HELP Committee to improve employment services for people with disabilities and support greater transition to competitive, integrated employment, with the eventual goal of ending sub-minimum wage and sheltered workshops.

### PREPARED STATEMENT OF THE NATIONAL INDUSTRIES FOR THE SEVERELY HANDICAPPED (NISH)

Mr. Chairman, Ranking Member, and members of the committee, thank you for the opportunity to submit this statement for the record for the September 15, 2011 roundtable on The Future of Employment for People with the Most Significant Disabilities.

As the committee reviews strategies to identify the right spectrum of employment options to address the needs of workers with the most significant disabilities, NISH shares the committee's objectives to increase earnings over time and promote career goals. NISH and the AbilityOne Program are proud of our strong record of accomplishments in providing employment with opportunities for upward mobility to tens of thousands of Americans. For our employees—and their friends and family members—the AbilityOne Program plays a vital, irreplaceable role in their lives.

The AbilityOne Program employs more than 47,000 Americans who are blind or have significant disabilities through government purchases of products and services provided by nonprofit agencies throughout the Nation. In 2010, NISH/AbilityOne nonprofit agencies employed 42,500 employees who earned an average hourly wage of $11.23. Participation in the AbilityOne Program further enabled these agencies to employ an additional 81,500 individuals with significant disabilities outside of the Program.

NISH/AbilityOne jobs are most often located in community-based, integrated settings including Federal buildings and military installations throughout our country. Additionally, a majority of these jobs provide wages that are generally higher than those found within the local communities and include health and other benefits. Employment through the AbilityOne Program empowers and encourages self-determination by enabling people with significant disabilities to make informed choices about key aspects of their employment. Nonprofit agencies affiliated with the AbilityOne Program utilize multiple employment options beyond the Program including customized employment and supported employment to provide work to people with the most significant disabilities.

It is also important to note that people with significant disabilities have a broad range of options with regard to their employment in the AbilityOne Program. These choices include competitive integrated employment, supported employment, and community group employment. The individual's desirable employment outcome should be selected through the informed choice of the individual with disabilities based on their unique talents, abilities, and interests, and not by others. NISH believes that we should continue to work collaboratively to ensure that a full range of employment options remains available for people with significant disabilities.

We take great pride in knowing that employment opportunities created through the AbilityOne Program have increased substantially over the last two decades. During this same time period, employment for people with significant disabilities in the commercial sector has remained flat or decreased slightly, while employment for people with significant disabilities in the Federal Government still remains too low. AbilityOne has thus provided an increasingly critical source of employment for individuals with significant disabilities at a time when alternative options have been diminishing or disappearing.

Together, AbilityOne and NISH have crafted dynamic strategic plans to address growing employment needs of our community. These plans include tactics that leverage state-of-the-art technologies and cutting-edge rehabilitation support services aimed at promoting upward mobility and independent community living goals for people with significant disabilities.

As an example, Marlon Wilkins of northern Virginia found a career through the AbilityOne Program. Mr. Wilkins has restricted mobility and partial paralysis from Transverse Myelitis. Thanks to the AbilityOne Program, Mr. Wilkins began his career at Linden Resources, Inc. as a document clerk working on the GSA Office of Transportation Audits contract. Within a few years he was promoted, eventually landing a supervisory role on the GSA contract. As supervisor, Mr. Wilkins was given responsibility for managing 300,000 billing documents and supporting information from approximately 730 Federal reporting activities each month. In 2008, he was promoted to assistant project manager on Linden's AbilityOne Bureau of Alcohol, Tobacco and Firearms (ATF) project. Under his leadership, the team maintained a 99 percent accuracy rate despite a backlog that occurred during a move that relocated the project to a new site. For Mr. Wilkins, not to mention his employers and coworkers, the mission of the AbilityOne Program has been a factor to achieving success and he recently stated the following:

"The program has offered various opportunities for personal growth. It's helped me advance to a project manager on one of Linden's largest contracts. I think the key to my success has been my drive, determination and most of all the managers I've worked with in the past and present. They have helped me improve my managerial skills. Without them giving me the opportunity for success, I wouldn't be where I am today."

NISH looks forward to continuing to work with Congress, the Administration, and the disability community to find solutions through a variety of strategies to the unacceptably low rate of employment for people with significant disabilities.

Thank you for considering our statement. Please feel free to contact John Kelly, Director of Government Affairs at *jkelly@nish.org* or (571) 226–4691 if you have any questions.

### SUPPLEMENTAL STATEMENT OF SERVICESOURCE

I appreciate the opportunity given to us by the U.S. Senate Committee on Health, Education, Labor, and Pensions (HELP) to give supplemental testimony in response to this important issue regarding employment for people with the most significant disabilities. The mission of ServiceSource is to provide exceptional services to individuals with disabilities through innovative and valued employment, training, habilitation, housing and support services. The not-for-profit corporation has regional offices and programs in nine States and the District of Columbia, annually providing job training and support services to over 13,000 people with disabilities annually.

ServiceSource operates a broad variety of employment and habilitation services, including job placement, group supported employment, center-based employment and community-based habilitation. As a leader in the disability field, ServiceSource develops strategic partnerships with community businesses, government entities and non-profit leaders to help bridge the gaps for individuals with disabilities and create sustainable opportunities that benefit the entire community and result in greater independence for the individual.

What follows is a personal life story from Mark Hall, ServiceSource, executive vice president, Corporate Development. A former business development and government relations manager within the California and northern Virginia aerospace industry, Mark re-directed his career 14 years ago when he joined our team here at ServiceSource. Mark and his wife Kathy have two children, including James, a 21-year-old son who has been diagnosed with Down syndrome. Mark tells the story of how he and his family have undergone an evolutionary process of understanding that all people with disabilities deserve the opportunity to be provided options in terms of employment and support. On the following pages, Mark offers his hopes for his son, James, to obtain a quality employment outcome and a satisfying, meaningful life.

**James Hall and a Life Moving Forward—*Including a Life History from His Dad!***

My name is Mark Hall and my wife Kathy and I are the parents of two children, James and Elizabeth. James, the older of the two, was born in 1989 in southern California and was immediately diagnosed with Down syndrome. To say the least, that diagnosis was an immediate life-changing experience as neither Kathy nor I had any previous life experience with anyone with a significant disability.

For the past 14 years, I have been an executive with ServiceSource of Alexandria, VA. ServiceSource is a nonprofit community rehabilitation program that today serves over 13,000 people with disabilities in nine States and the District of Columbia. I am responsible for business and program development for the organization, to enhance rehabilitation programs and develop new employment opportunities for people with disabilities.

Although James and his disability were new to us when he was born, we knew we had to quickly get smart about Down syndrome. Both Kathy and I consider ourselves well-educated as we share three Masters Degrees between us. We knew right away that we would have to do our best to learn about treatments and therapies for our son. Soon after James was diagnosed, we began reading and attending conferences to learn more about Down syndrome. One early conference was a life-saver for James as we learned that all babies with Down syndrome should undergo a heart echocardiogram. James' pediatrician didn't believe that James had a heart condition that warranted this procedure, but he agreed to write a prescription when we insisted. The echocardiogram revealed that James had a significant heart defect that required open heart surgery before his first birthday. We learned early on that we held a new responsibility of advocating for James in his life.

Our family moved to Virginia in 1991 when the decline of the southern California aerospace industry necessitated that I apply my business development capabilities in new markets outside of national defense. I was able to stay with my employer and move into a new position that involved business development and government relations for nuclear waste disposal and automated finger identification—a significant change from my defense background. An added benefit of that move meant that Kathy was able to leave the workforce and devote her time to being a mother and a homemaker to our two children.

As an infant with Down syndrome in Fairfax County, James was provided very high-quality intervention services through the school system. Although he experienced significant delays in speech, mobility and eating skills, he was a happy and loving child. A highlight for him was learning to swim when he was 2 years old, a milestone that occurred before he could walk on his own. Today, one of James' favorite activities is swimming laps and jumping off the diving board.

Looking back, we were fortunate that James received his early intervention services at our neighborhood elementary school and over time we grew comfortable with the setting and the school staff. Because of his delays, we made the decision to hold back James from kindergarten until he was 6 years old. During his preschool years, by attending several conferences, we also learned about and became enthusiastic supporters of full inclusion for children with disabilities in our schools.

As Kathy and I discussed kindergarten placement with the school system for James, it rapidly became apparent that if left to the school administrators, James would not be programmed into our neighborhood school, but instead would be bussed to another elementary school 5 miles from our home. His placement would be a segregated special education classroom with other children with intellectual disabilities. This was the recommendation despite the broad range of special education services that were provided to children with learning disabilities at our neighborhood school. Both Kathy and I stood firm that James could and would receive special education services in an inclusive environment in our neighborhood school. He believed that it was his right to ride the school bus along with Elizabeth and other children on our block.

To support that goal, and over a period of almost 2 years, we worked together with other parents and advocates in Fairfax County to promote more inclusive schools. We formed a parent advocacy group, *Neighborhood School Now*, and immediately our group sought community and media attention. We met with senior school officials and lobbied the school board. We were enthusiastic and vocal in our advocacy. Ever so slowly we made progress and we began to see the school system move toward more inclusion on a child-by-child basis.

James' elementary school placement was in question until the Friday before the 1995 Labor Day weekend. Finally, that Thursday, the local community newspaper ran its weekly edition with a front-page story on James and our family and our desire for him to attend his neighborhood school. The article was well-researched and the reporter compellingly presented our case. That Friday morning after the newspaper story was published, I received a phone call from the principal at our neighborhood school and she told me that James would be welcome to attend her school the following Tuesday, the first day of the new school year. As far as we know, James Hall was the first child diagnosed with Down syndrome to be fully included in Fairfax County's school system.

That first school day began a period where James was fully included with his peers without disabilities at our neighborhood school. He rode the bus to school with his sister and other neighborhood children—even though he continued to be offered special education transportation every year. He received support services in the classroom and only left class for additional speech and occupational therapy. Although there were some bumps along the road, James thrived in elementary school and had a very positive experience. He learned to read at the second-grade level and participated at an appropriate level in most of the curriculum. Besides school, James was active at our church and rose to the rank of Webelo in the Cub Scouts as a fully included member of his den and pack.

Also during that period of time, in addition to my activities with *Neighborhood Schools Now*, I was nominated by the ServiceSource Chairman of the Board and my supervisor at my regular employer to join the ServiceSource Board of Directors. In 1996, I was nominated and selected for the Brookings Congressional Fellowship program that resulted in a 9-month fellowship with Senate Majority Leader Trent Lott. By being in the right place at the right time, I volunteered to be assigned to the bipartisan team that was working on the reauthorization of the Individuals with Disabilities Act (IDEA) that was eventually signed into law in 1997. The opportunity for me to make a very small contribution to the passage of that legislation while meeting others with a commitment and passion for assisting people with disabilities was an experience that made me realize that I wanted to do something more with my life than worry about the future of nuclear waste disposal. After concluding my congressional fellowship and much to my employer's chagrin, I approached Janet Samuelson, president and CEO of ServiceSource, and suggested that she add me to her team to help with the organization's marketing effort. She agreed, offered me a job and I joined the ServiceSource staff in late 1997 and I have never regretted the move.

On the home front, James progressed through elementary school without any major incidents or problems; we overcame the minor issues he faced with good planning and hard work. James did very well in elementary school, and some might say that he was a model student for full inclusion.

However, when James finished elementary school and began his middle school and high school years, his educational experience grew more difficult. His transition to our neighborhood middle school was very traumatic and caused James a great deal of stress. James began acting out in the classroom and stopped talking both at home and at school. We witnessed a large increase in a variety of compulsive behaviors and routines, and James stopped eating at the table with the family during mealtimes. Although he had sometimes done this earlier, he greatly escalated tossing and throwing nearby items when put into environments or transitions he did not understand. He regressed in his life skills and he obviously was not a happy young man. Eventually Kathy and I recognized that these issues were not getting better through behavior modification and other strategies, so we began seeing Dr. George Capone at the Kennedy Krieger Institute located at Johns Hopkins in Baltimore, Maryland.

All attempts to have James fully included ceased in fall of 2005 when James began attending Chantilly High School. The school offered a traditional segregated special education program and although philosophically was not our first choice for James, he responded well and after his first year, he found a routine and began to settle down. Also while at high school, he has had the opportunity to participate in a variety of work experiences including working at a hotel laundry, a computer recycling facility, a thrift store and some mail delivery work. He has enjoyed each of those experiences.

Since he was 18, James has been receiving SSDI payments. The local community service board has identified him as Medicaid waiver eligible. In general, he has no comprehension of money and it is not a motivator for him, so wage rates (including minimum wage) are not an issue as Kathy and I are committed to meeting his needs. He is non-verbal and often exhibits inappropriate behaviors including throwing items when he is faced with a disappointment or experiences rapid change. James also requires coaching to complete life's basic tasks including personal hygiene, eating and getting dressed.

Today, James is 21 years old and is a nice young man with a wry sense of humor. He is now in his last year in the Fairfax County school system, where he has been receiving services since he was 2 years old. Over the past few years and as part of his school curriculum, he has been receiving transition planning services. James' sister, Elizabeth, is a 20-year-old Junior at the College of William and Mary and she helps keep track of James too. For the foreseeable future, Kathy and I expect James to live with us at our home.

Our family is thinking about James' future and we are hopeful that he can be served by ServiceSource as he moves into adulthood.

As James has grown into becoming a young man, both Kathy and I have modified our thoughts and feelings about full inclusion for him as we realize his level of ability and what he wants in his own life. We are very interested in James becoming a contributing adult and that he continues to develop a feeling of accomplishment and self worth. However, as James' parents, we are mindful that James will require a high degree of ongoing supports in order for him to work and live. For the future, we are hopeful that James can develop a lifestyle that brings him happiness, safety and a sense of well-being. As James' legal guardians, Kathy and I are seeking an employment outcome for him that will keep James positively occupied and provide him with a fulfilling life. At this point in time, we anticipate that James will not be competitively employable, and that he will need continued ongoing supports to function as an adult.

I fully realize that my thoughts about inclusion have evolved from my thinking when James was entering kindergarten. Whereas, I once was a loud and perhaps obnoxious proponent for full inclusion, I am now more moderate in my thinking. I recognize that inclusion and competitive community employment may not be the best outcome for all individuals with disabilities—some people require a greater level and more intensive support to succeed. As Kathy and I work together with James and the many people that provide him with support, we are mindful that it is best to have a broad range of options to consider. Those options for James might include center-based or day habilitation services as well as group-supported or community-based employment.

As all parents of children with disabilities are prone to do, we worry about James' long-term future when we are gone. We do have hope that James will continue to grow in his skill development and will find an employment outcome that will provide him with a sense of safety and well-being. We are excited about the changing world for people with disabilities. Almost every day we learn about new opportunities and accomplishments for people with disabilities. We are confident that over time, James will have a variety of opportunities for him to experience a happy and productive life. We love James and are very grateful that he is part of our lives.

PREPARED STATEMENT OF LAURA WALLING, DIRECTOR, ADVOCACY AND LEGISLATIVE AFFAIRS, GOODWILL INDUSTRIES INTERNATIONAL

Mr. Chairman, Ranking Member, and members of the committee, on behalf of Goodwill Industries International, Inc., I appreciate this opportunity to submit a written statement for the record on the important issue of the future of employment of people with significant disabilities. Goodwill Industries® applauds the committee for its interest and leadership in examining this topic. Goodwill® believes that work is a valued activity that allows people to participate in the mainstream of life. Sadly, job opportunities for people with significant disabilities are limited, and they would be even more limited if not for special provisions provided in Federal law and center-based programs.

Goodwill Industries is comprised of 158 independent, community-based Goodwill agencies in the United States. Goodwill's network of local agencies provided employment training, job placement services and other community services to nearly 2.5 million people last year. Over 240,000 of those individuals reported to have a disabling condition. In addition, 170,000 people obtained meaningful employment as a result of Goodwill career services programs. Collectively, these employees earned $2.7 billion in salaries and wages and contribute to their communities as productive, taxpaying citizens.

Goodwill agencies help to fund programs by selling donated clothes and other household items at more than 2,500 donated goods retail stores and online at *shopgoodwill.com*. Many people with disabilities work in Goodwill stores. In addition, Goodwill agencies employ people with disabilities and other employment challenges in the delivery of a wide variety of quality commercial services that are contracted to community partners, business, and government. People employed by Goodwill contracting services work in industries including customer relations, administrative support, document management, office administration, packaging and assembly, food service preparation, custodial services, and groundskeeping.

Over 75 community-based Goodwill agencies collectively engage more than 7,000 individuals with disabilities to fulfill more than 350 AbilityOne contracts, while offering those workers job coaching and additional skills training. The AbilityOne program is the largest provider of employment opportunities for those who are either blind or have significant disabilities, employing approximately 46,000 people through more than 600 nonprofit agencies.

The workforce development services provided to people with disabilities include: intake/eligibility; work assessment/evaluation; job readiness/soft-skills training/work adjustment; occupational skills training; on-the-job training (both inside and outside of Goodwill); intensive placement services sessions; supported employment; and e-learning among others.

### EMPLOYMENT OPTIONS

During the discussion, Chairman Harkin asked the panel, "What is the right spectrum of employment options that will address the needs of workers with the most significant disabilities?" Goodwill believes that all individuals should have the choice to work in the employment setting that they desire and that no one should be denied the opportunity to work and receive the intangible benefits of work—independence, participation in society, dignity, self-esteem, and sense of accomplishment among others. When considering the full range of options for individuals, center-based employment should not be viewed as a place of last resort. For some individuals, center-based employment may be an appropriate option that they and their guardians should be allowed to consider.

### EMPLOYMENT STRATEGIES

A second topic raised by Chairman Harkin pertained to employment strategies. Specifically the panel was asked, "What are the most effective and proven strategies to help workers achieve the highest pay and advance in their careers?" With congressional leadership, Goodwill Industries believes that we can and must move forward to eliminate the barriers that prevent people with disabilities from participating in the workforce. In addition to exposing individuals to all of the employment options before them, strong relationships with employers are important to achieve the goal of increasing the number of people with significant disabilities in the workforce. The autonomous, community-based structure of Goodwill Industries allows for agencies to have strong relationships with local employers, resulting in increased opportunities for individuals served to find a job and advance in careers.

Goodwill Industries has put forth specific recommendations in the past related to increased oversight and enforcement of the Fair Labor Standards Act and the great need to reauthorize the Workforce Investment Act. As producers within the AbilityOne program, many Goodwill agencies have been early adopters of the AbilityOne Quality Work Environment (QWE) initiative. QWE is, "a strategy through which key stakeholders in the AbilityOne Program will collaborate to identify and implement best practices in the [nonprofit] work environments that will enable people who are blind or have significant disabilities to achieve their maximum employment potential through opportunities to do the work of their choice; a strategy to empower AbilityOne producing NPAs to make improvements in key areas of the work environment, thus strengthening experience, productivity, and opportunity for all.

### CONCLUSION

Thank you for your continued leadership on this issue. We look forward to working with Congress to consider legislative changes that will increase employment opportunities for people with disabilities.

————

SEPTEMBER 25, 2011.

Senator TOM HARKIN,
*731 Hart Senate Building,*
*Washington, DC 20510.*

DEAR SENATOR HARKIN, I would like to thank you for the opportunity to participate in your roundtable discussion on September 15, 2011 regarding employment for persons with severe disabilities.

As you recall I am a parent of a young man who has severe intellectual disabilities. When Josh was young, our goal for him was to live in his own home and to work in our community. Three and a half years ago, Josh moved into his own home with 24 hour support through the Intellectual Disability Title IX waiver program. He accesses the Consumer Choice Option program that allows me to manage his services, thus allowing a great deal of flexibility for his services. Josh is having a great deal of success and he is very happy and content with his life. Josh spends his days at Tenco, our local sheltered workshop and he participates in the day habilitation program. Due to the level of supervision that Josh requires, he is not able to work even at the sheltered workshop. Almost a year ago, I was able to convince his team to allow me to hire someone through the Consumer Choice Options program to allow Josh to work a few hours per week while at Tenco. He shreds paper with the assistance of his one-on-one staff person. Without an increase in his budget, he can only work a few hours per week. The few hours that Josh does work, means a great deal to him and as a result, his behaviors have improved and he is less anxious and more content. Josh is only able to work as a result of the flexibility that is allowed through the Consumer Choice Option program and adding to his budget would allow him the opportunity to work additional hours.

My goal has always been for Josh to work in our community and I would love to see that happen. I have always been told that Josh is not eligible for supported employment services as he would need the service long term. I just don't see how my goal of Josh working in our community can ever happen due to the level of supervision that he requires. In our community those individuals who do participate in supported employment services are generally only able to work 4 to 6 hours per week. Josh spends 30 hours per week at Tenco and he is surrounded by friends and a good support team. He would not be happy only having something to do 4 to 6 hours per week.

Until Supported Employment service guidelines are changed and become more flexible, sheltered workshop programs need to remain in place to allow individuals with severe intellectual disabilities to be involved in a program that allows them activities to occupy their day.

Again, thank you for the opportunity to be a part of your roundtable discussion. It was a once in a life time opportunity for a long term advocate and I thoroughly enjoyed the experience.

Best Regards,

DEB PUMPHREY,
*Parent Advocate, Ottumwa, IA.*

––––––––

CONSORTIUM OF CITIZENS WITH DISABILITIES EMPLOYMENT AND
TRAINING TASK FORCE,
*September 29, 2011.*

Hon. TOM HARKIN, *Chairman,*
*Health, Education, Labor, and Pensions Committee,*
*U.S. Senate,*
*Washington, DC 20510.*

Hon. MIKE ENZI, *Ranking Member,*
*Health, Education, Labor, and Pensions Committee,*
*U.S. Senate,*
*Washington, DC 20510.*

DEAR SENATORS HARKIN AND ENZI: On behalf of the Consortium of Citizens with Disabilities Employment and Training Task Force, we appreciate your sponsorship of the September 15, 2011 roundtable on *The Future of Employment for People with the Most Significant Disabilities.* The Consortium of Citizens with Disabilities is a coalition of more than 130 national disability-related organizations working together to advocate for national public policy that ensures full equality, self-determination, independence, empowerment, integration and inclusion of children and adults with disabilities in all aspects of society.

Because the record for submission of comments was only recently opened to the general public beyond the roundtable participants, we have not had time to produce comments specifically tailored to the particular issues addressed on September 15. However, our task force was asked to testify before the House Ways and Means Social Security and Human Resources Subcommittees on September 23d on Social Security disability program work disincentives. We believe that the recommendations provided in that testimony may be of use to your committee and attach it with this cover email for your information.

The CCD Employment and Training Task Force believes that meaningful employment represents one of the best opportunities for people with disabilities as they work toward becoming a productive and independent member in their community. To that end, we applaud your continued efforts to address the deplorable state of workforce participation among Americans with disabilities.

Our task force believes that employment of individuals with disabilities requires a comprehensive approach that addresses all aspects of the service system to ensure that the vision of integrated, competitive employment is fostered and promoted. Ongoing staff development, among systems staff and service providers, is vital so that they not only embrace this vision, but also have the technical knowledge to implement it. A holistic approach also requires addressing a wide range of other issues: outreach to and engagement with employers, service monitoring and quality assurance, engagement of individuals and families, the availability of benefits counseling that supports community employment, transportation, inter-agency collaboration with public vocational rehabilitation, to name just a few. Strong transition services from school-to-work, with a clear focus on community employment are also critical.

Our specific recommendations pertain to urgently needed renewals of several critical work incentives programs and improvements that can be made to the Ticket to Work and Work Incentives Improvement Act (TTWWIIA). While we recognize that much of TTWWIIA falls within the jurisdiction of another committee, we also know that you understand the necessity for breaking down the unnecessary *silos* that exist in Washington that create impediments to true progress in advancing employment of people with disabilities.

We are also concerned about maintaining and enhancing the health care coverage that has been provided to thousands of working people with disabilities through the Medicaid Buy-Ins, extension of premium free Medicare and provisions of the Affordable Health Care Act (ACA). The development of regulations implementing the health exchanges and essential benefits packages under the ACA could determine whether progress made to date is advanced or undermined and we urge your attention to this critical piece of the disability work incentives puzzle.

If the HELP Committee is truly committed to removing barriers to work for people with significant disabilities, then it must move Congress to address those impediments that continue in Social Security Title II and Title XVI programs. Social Security disability beneficiaries continue to grapple with the complexities of the benefit system, with the fear of sudden termination of benefits without an easy return to the rolls if their condition necessitates that, and with outmoded asset and income disregards that dampen initiative and punish success.

Finally, there are disability tax credits and deductions that need to be modernized and business tax incentives that must be renewed if people with disabilities are to enter the mainstream of the American labor force. As Congress turns its attention to reform of the tax code, we urge you not to forget changes that can aid the employment of people with disabilities.

We thank you for your attention to these comments and welcome the opportunity to support your committee in its efforts to advance economic self-sufficiency for Americans with disabilities.

CHERYL BATES-HARRIS,
*Co-chair, NDRN.*

ALICIA EPSTEIN,
*Co-chair, NISH.*

SUSAN GOODMAN,
*Co-chair, APSE and National Down Syndrome Congress.*

CHARLIE HARLES,
*Co-chair, International Association of Business, Industry and Rehabilitation.*

SUSAN PROKOP,
*Co-chair, Paralyzed Veterans of America.*

PAUL SEIFERT,
*Co-chair, Council of State Administrators for Vocational Rehabilitation.*

[Whereupon, at 12:10 p.m., the hearing was adjourned.]

○